"An excellent mix of quantitative tools and in-depth examples"
> FRANCIS A. LONGSTAFF
> Allstate Professor of Insurance and Finance,
> UCLA Anderson School of Management

"The rapid development of derivatives on credit products in the last decade has greatly facilitated the ability of participants in global capital markets to efficiently exchange credit risk. This has contributed to economic growth by increasing the efficiency of the market for users of capital. The insights into the latest evolutions of these products, contained in this book, provide an invaluable resource for a broad range of market participants and observers."
> STEPHEN WEST
> Founding Partner, TriPoint Asset Management

"*Credit Derivative Strategies* meets the challenge of bringing financial analysts and risk managers up to date on valuation, risk assessment, and product design in the fast-moving market for credit derivatives. The chapters are well selected for a mix of pragmatic institutional knowledge, conceptual frameworks, and technical foundations. I recommend it highly."
> DARRELL DUFFIE
> Dean Witter Distinguished Professor of Finance, Codirector of the
> Credit Risk Executive Program, Graduate School of Business,
> Stanford University

Credit
Derivative
Strategies

Credit
Derivative
Strategies

New Thinking on
Managing Risk and Return

EDITED BY

Rohan Douglas

BLOOMBERG PRESS
NEW YORK

The Chartered Financial Analyst® (CFA®) designation is a globally recognized standard for measuring the competence and integrity of investment professionals.

This publication contains the authors' opinions and is designed to provide accurate and authoritative information. It is sold with the understanding that the authors, publisher, and Bloomberg L.P. are not engaged in rendering legal, accounting, investment-planning, or other professional advice. The reader should seek the services of a qualified professional for such advice; the authors, publisher, and Bloomberg L.P. cannot be held responsible for any loss incurred as a result of specific investments or planning decisions made by the reader.

First edition published 2007
1 3 5 7 9 10 8 6 4 2

Library of Congress Cataloging-in-Publication Data

Credit derivative strategies : new thinking on managing risk and return / edited by Rohan Douglas.
 p. cm.
 Summary: "Credit Derivatives are financial contracts that transfer credit risk--the risk that a debtor will not repay a loan--between parties. Credit Derivative Strategies describes for professional investors current ways of participating in this rapidly expanding market, including how to select credit hedge funds, analyze event risk, find relative value opportunities, and choose synthetic collateralized debt obligations (CDOs)"--Provided by publisher.
 Includes bibliographical references and index.
 ISBN 978-1-57660-187-7 (alk. paper)
 1. Credit derivatives. 2. Risk management. I. Douglas, Rohan.

HG6024.A3C737 2007
332.63'2--dc22   2007014284

CONTENTS

Rohan Douglas, editor of this volume, is the founder and CEO of Quantifi Inc., a leading provider of pricing models and risk analysis tools for structured credit. He has more than twenty-five years of experience in the global financial industry. Prior to founding Quantifi, he was the director of global credit derivatives research at Citigroup and Salomon Smith Barney where he worked for ten years. Douglas has worked in interest-rate derivatives, emerging markets, and global fixed income. Douglas is also an adjunct professor in the financial engineering program at Polytechnic University in New York and at the Macquarie University Applied Finance Centre in Australia and Singapore. For many years, Douglas has spoken at conferences and seminars on the subject of credit derivatives.

Santa Federico is the chief risk officer for Perry Capital, a $13 billion multistrategy hedge fund. Prior to working at Perry Capital, he was managing director of strategic risk management at Credit Suisse First Boston and head market risk manager for Salomon Smith Barney/Citigroup. Besides risk management, he has held various positions in portfolio management, derivatives trading, and quantitative research. He has twenty years of financial industry experience and holds degrees in physics from Princeton University and the École Centrale de Paris.

Alla Gil has fourteen years of financial experience working at major banks, such as Citigroup, Goldman Sachs, and CIBC. Most recently, she was the managing director of International Capital Solutions Group for Nomura Securities International. Her group developed innovative and practical financial solutions by quantifying clients' exposures to different risk facets and identifying the most efficient risk mitigation strategies.

Richard Horwitz is the managing director of manager assessment and risk management of Merrill Lynch's Hedge Fund Development and Management Group (HFDMG). He has implemented Risk Fundamentals, a proprietary risk transparency and management system. He was formerly a senior vice president of risk management and investment analytics at Kenmar Global Investment Management Inc., a $2 billion fund of funds. Horwitz previously worked as a principal and research analyst for Capital Market Risk Advisors, Sanford C. Bernstein & Co., and Booz Allen & Hamilton, Inc. He is also the author of *Hedge Fund Risk Fundamentals: Solving the Risk Management and Transparency Challenge*, published by Bloomberg Press in 2004.

Vivek Kapoor is an executive director at UBS, responsible for analyzing structured credit trading for UBS's alternative investment management business, Dillon Read Capital Management. His central focus is evaluating trading and hedging strategies and developing relative value metrics that are cognizant of the limits of replication. Prior to working at UBS, he was the risk manager for CDO trading at Credit Suisse where he was responsible for analyzing and communicating the risk-return profile of CDO trading. He obtained his PhD from the Massachusetts Institute of Technology in the area of stochastic modeling of geophysical flows and solute dispersion.

Christoph Klein, CFA, is the head of credit fixed income and a partner of TriPoint Asset Management, which manages a multistrategy hedge fund. He was formerly the director of portfolio management at CPM Advisors Limited, where he managed a multistrategy credit hedge fund and was responsible for issuer credit analysis and instrument selection. Before that, Klein was portfolio manager for corporate and convertible bond mandates at Deutsche Asset Management in Frankfurt. He is currently pursuing a PhD at Trier University, and wrote the chapter "Analysis and Evaluation of Corporate Bonds" for the *Handbook of European Fixed Income Securities*.

Steven D. Persky has more than twenty-five years of professional investment experience. In 1998, he cofounded Dalton Investments with Jamie Rosenwald and managed Dalton's distressed debt funds. He oversees U. S. operations for Dalton Investments LLC and serves as risk manager as well as manages Dalton's Private Client Services, which provide investment counseling and investment management to high-net-worth clients. Prior to founding Dalton, he was a vice president at Payden & Rygel, a Los Angeles-based investment advisory where he managed institutional fixed-income portfolios. He also worked for Salomon Brothers in New York and Tokyo in the fixed-income trading division. Persky holds an AB from Harvard

College (1980) where he majored in Asian Studies. He is a CFA charter holder (1994) and a member of the CFA Society of Los Angeles, Inc. and the CFA Institute.

Andrea Petrelli is the director of CDO trading risk management for Europe at Credit Suisse in London. His focus is portfolio credit derivatives valuation and risk modeling, and credit correlation. Prior to this, he worked at Banca Intesa, a major Italian bank, where his work was mainly devoted to credit derivatives modeling. He graduated from the University of Pisa where he also obtained his PhD in theoretical physics. He wrote his thesis on perturbative quantum chromodynamics at the CERN TH Division.

Peter Rivera is currently the department head of Business Technologies at the State University of New York in Dutchess County. After working as a certified public accountant, programmer, and mortgage securities trader, Rivera's career in credit risk management began when he joined a quantitative risk group within Bankers Trust's credit department in 1988. He joined Salomon Brothers in a similar capacity in 1993, and in 1997 accepted a position at Deutsche Bank as managing director responsible for managing the credit risk of all traded products as well as the RAROC methodology for customer-level and firm-wide credit risk. In 2002, he established Theory & Reality Risk Management to provide consulting and training in credit risk management. Rivera has a BS in accounting from Fordham University and an MBA in finance from New York University.

Erin Roye Simpson joined Merrill Lynch in February 2006, to perform risk analysis and aid in the development and implementation of risk-management tools in the Hedge Fund Development and Management Group. Prior to joining Merrill, she spent a year and a half at the Kenmar Fund as a member of the research team, where she performed quantitative research and aided in portfolio construction. She developed a system that helps construct portfolios and better understand portfolio risk. She graduated with honors from Yale University with a BS in astrophysics and has an MS in information and telecommunication systems from Johns Hopkins University.

Jun Zhang is the head of CDO risk management for the United States at Credit Suisse. He monitors risk for both synthetic and cash CDOs, such as spread, default, and correlation risks. Before joining Credit Suisse, he was a credit-risk quantitative analyst at Tokyo Mitsubishi Financial Group where he performed portfolio analysis of credit derivatives products. He speaks regularly at trading and risk management conferences. He holds a BS in engineering from Shanghai Jiao Tong University in China, an MS in mathematics in finance from New York University, and a PhD in engineering from Johns Hopkins University.

INTRODUCTION

ROHAN DOUGLAS

CREDIT DERIVATIVES are a relatively recent innovation, but they have already dramatically altered the playing field in finance. From origins in the U.S. high-yield market in the late 1980s and emerging markets in the early 1990s, the global credit derivatives market has roughly doubled each year, reaching an estimated $34.5 trillion notional outstanding as of the end of 2006.[1] It is useful, however, to put the size of this market in perspective: it is still only one-tenth the size of the global interest-rate derivatives market and has a huge potential for future growth.

Credit derivatives are financial contracts whose value is derived primarily from an underlying asset or market quote that incorporates credit risk. Credit derivatives come in many shapes and forms and continue to evolve rapidly. Some are structured like bonds or notes (funded), and some are structured like swaps (unfunded). The payoff can be any function of a wide variety of underlying assets or market quotes including bonds or loans, credit spreads, ratings, or defaults. Credit derivatives are primarily over-the-counter products, but exchange-traded contracts have been introduced. What is common among all these forms is that their primary purpose is the transfer of credit risk from one party to another.

The existence of a market for credit derivatives has fundamentally changed the way institutions manage money. Credit derivatives give banks new ways to manage their loan portfolios, give insurance companies and asset managers new investment vehicles, give hedge funds new opportunities, and give every part of the financial system a new way to transfer and manage credit risk.

Every year the financial community creates many innovative ways to use credit derivatives. Current applications include:
- ❏ Market making
- ❏ Reduction or management of regulatory and economic capital

❑ Trading opportunities including
  —Leveraged returns or yield enhancement
  —Arbitrage opportunities
  —Access to alternate markets
  —Efficient expressions of credit view including shorts
❑ Risk management including
  —Reduction or management of credit line usage
  —Management of individual credit exposures
  —Diversification of portfolio risk

In the beginning, most participants in the global market for credit derivatives were money center banks. Next to enter were reinsurers, and then came the hedge funds. Insurance companies and asset managers are the most recent entrants. The market now includes a rich mix of investors and speculators and becomes deeper and more balanced with each passing year.

As the applications for credit derivatives have grown, so has the need for more information about the market. While there have been many good sources of "product" information, there have been far fewer sources for practical information about investment strategies.

This book is intended to redress that imbalance by exploring some of the practical and applied issues involved in investing in credit derivatives.

The book is organized "in reverse" so to speak, with introductory material placed at the end of the book as a reference. This allows the more advanced reader to proceed with the most relevant and interesting work at the start of the book.

All potential investors ask: "How do I choose among the many investments and strategies?"

Part One of this book, "Investment Strategies," addresses this question. Each chapter gives the reader practical and real-world examples of different investment strategies currently used by market participants.

In Chapter 1, "Eight Relative Value Opportunities," Christoph Klein surveys many of the trading strategies currently employed by multistrategy hedge funds. Steven D. Persky in Chapter 2, "Distressed Debt Strategies," gives a very clear and concise set of examples of distressed debt strategies from the Asian, CBO, and Latin American markets—markets in which he has a long history. Chapter 3, "Four Synthetic CDO Trading Strategies," by Andrea Petrelli, Jun Zhang, Santa Federico, and Vivek Kapoor compares the risks and rewards of several synthetic CDO strategies. This is a complex subject but one that offers many investment opportunities. In Chapter 4, "Integrating Credit Hedge Funds into a Portfolio of Investments," Richard Horwitz and Erin Roye Simpson outline an approach for incorporating credit into a broadly diversified portfolio.

Transference of credit risk is what makes credit derivatives unique. Measurement and management of this credit risk introduces many unique challenges.

Part Two, "Risk Management Strategies," focuses on the issues relating to the risk management of credit derivatives.

In Chapter 5, "Risk Management of Credit Derivatives," Santa Federico, Andrea Petrelli, Jun Zhang, and Vivek Kapoor outline the basics of credit risk management using examples from the CDO market. Christoph Klein, the author of Chapter 1, turns to a related subject in Chapter 6, "Risk Management for Multistrategy Funds." In this chapter, Klein reviews the risk management challenges faced by multistrategy credit funds and suggests practical approaches to resolve them. Klein shows what risk management is necessary to manage the investment strategies he outlined in Chapter 1. Alla Gil details a new approach for analyzing risks in Chapter 7, "Integrating Event Risk in Portfolio Construction." The limitations of VaR when applied to portfolios including credit are well-known. Here, Gil introduces a natural extension of VaR, which incorporates the increased likelihood of extreme events (fat tails) observed in the credit markets. In addition, this new measure can be used to facilitate portfolio optimization for diverse portfolios including credit derivatives.

Since the beginning of the credit derivatives market, pricing and valuation has been a particular challenge. Multiasset credit derivatives, in particular, have proved to be one of the most interesting and difficult areas of quantitative research. Despite the challenges, a considerable amount of focus and development has resulted in a steady and consistent improvement and evolution in the models and what is considered best practice for credit derivative pricing.

Part Three, "Pricing, Products, and Procedures," is a road map to the most important pricing concepts and a starting point for exploration of this topic.

In Chapter 8, "Pricing Models," Peter Rivera and I describe the most widely used credit models and how to apply them. In Chapter 9, "CDS Valuation," Santa Federico, Andrea Petrelli, Jun Zhang, and Vivek Kapoor detail the "market standard" pricing of credit default swaps along with some of the more common sensitivity measures. Santa Federico, Andrea Petrelli, Jun Zhang, and Vivek Kapoor contribute once again on the subject of CDOs. In Chapter 10, "CDO Valuation," they describe two variations (Fourier transform and recursive) of time-to-default copula models, which are the current "market standard" for pricing CDOs. In Chapter 11, "Credit Derivative Products," Peter Rivera explains the mechanics of some of the more common credit derivative products.

Notes

1. ISDA Year-End 2006 Market Survey.

PART ONE

INVESTMENT STRATEGIES

CHAPTER 1

Eight Relative Value Opportunities

CHRISTOPH KLEIN

This chapter describes credit-relative value trades from the perspective of a multistrategy credit hedge fund. The following chapters will describe all credit instruments in more detail.

A multistrategy framework confers important advantages to a fund. It allows the fund to dynamically exploit a wide range of market situations, integrate new credit instruments as they are developed, and create a diversified portfolio, which is more likely to generate stable and attractive risk-adjusted returns over time.

The model for this discussion is a multistrategy credit hedge fund, which seeks to systematically exploit inefficiencies in credit markets using cash and derivative instruments. The focus is on primarily corporate bonds, credit derivatives, and credit index products; but it can also invest in structured products (collateralized debt obligations, or CDOs, and first-to-default baskets), convertible bonds, loans and their derivatives, and equities (as part of capital structure trades).

The cornerstone of this multistrategy approach is an investment strategy that emphasizes a thorough credit analysis. Accordingly, this chapter begins with an overview of the credit analysis process that forms the basis for generating trade ideas.

The primary focus of this chapter will be to describe briefly eight investment strategies with mechanics, rationale, and trade examples.

Chapter 6 delivers an overview of the portfolio risk management process for a multistrategy approach including the allocation process among the strategies.

The Investment Process

The task of a credit hedge fund is to generate attractive returns from all credit and credit-related products while reducing the portfolio risk by use of appropriate hedging strategies.

Most investment ideas are based on a *bottom-up* approach, characterized by a thorough fundamental analysis of the underlying particulars of the instrument. The fundamental objective is to forecast an issuer's credit risk, and whether this is in an improving or deteriorating trend, using a process that is efficient, transparent, and reliable. The weighting of the different investment strategies and any portfolio biases and factor risk exposures, such as net issuer sector weighting or net credit market exposure, are assessed and possibly adjusted. (These factor risks are explained in Chapter 6). These assessments are performed in a top-down corrective process, which considers macroeconomic input factors on a regular basis.

The credit process starts with idea generation from daily empirical output and filtered constant news flow, portfolio manager experience, industry contacts, and other well-developed relationships in and beyond the capital markets community. After ideas are generated, the further investment process includes issuer research supported by internal sector rating models based on discriminant analysis and careful instrument selection and trade execution.

The factors in the sector credit rating models are fundamentally preselected and cover different balance sheet, income statement, and cash flow statement analysis areas, such as leverage, interest expense coverage, and free cash flow growth. In addition, Merton-type credit evaluation models can be used, which could be based on equity volatility, balance sheet data, and spread movements.[1] The significance and the directional similarity of the model outputs are checked for every issuer. After this screening, an internal credit rating is performed.

Internal Credit Rating

Efficient quantitative credit rating models for different industry sectors are developed using discriminant analysis. These quantitative outputs are the basis for determining an internal credit rating. Briefly, discriminant analysis is a statistical technique that takes a series of informational inputs and reduces them to a single number.[2] A general discriminant model can be described as:

$$A \times a + B \times b + \ldots + N \times n = X$$

Where:

A … *N* are variables (for example, debt-equity ratio)
a … *n* are discriminant coefficients or factor loads
X is the output

In the context of credit analysis, *A* … *N*, the informational inputs, are typically financial ratios. For example, important ratios for industrial corporations include free cash flow to total debt, the inverse of the variation coefficient of operating cash flows (an indicator of the stability of cash flows) and retained earnings to total assets. Additionally, market capitalization, which is a monetary value rather than a ratio, is an indicator of a corporate's size.

Carefully controlled discriminant analysis generates the discriminant coefficients, *a* … *n* and indicates the relative importance of each of the informational inputs. In order to achieve reliable and fundamentally sound results, it is important to state a fundamental hypothesis regarding the relationship (positive or negative) of the input to the output prior to including a variable.

The output, *X*, is a number that can be scaled to an equivalent credit rating. This calibration of a model score into a rating agency's rating notch equivalent is an important step for practical usage.

The objective is to have as reliable an output as possible with the smallest number of inputs. This also ensures efficiency and transparency. As a result, developing and calibrating a reliable model is as much, if not more, an art as pure science. Insofar as companies in different industries may be affected by factors differently, individual discriminant analysis models are typically developed for each industry. Additionally, they must be constantly reevaluated to ensure long-term reliability.

These models conduct stress tests (for example, plugging in expected values for all model ratios assuming a debt-financed acquisition), and, more importantly, new relevant information can be used to quickly adjust the internal rating estimates.

Qualitative Factors

The quantitatively derived internal ratings described previously are only the first step in the analysis.[3] The internal research focuses on various interrelated micro and macro themes:

❏ *Where are we in the credit cycle?* Overview of default and recovery rates in the context of historical statistics and in relation to other sectors

 ❏ *Current rating trends*
 ❏ *Industry characteristics and strategies.* Focuses on the level of

competitiveness and barriers to entry through the use of approaches such as the Porter model and SWOT (strengths, weaknesses, opportunities and threats) analysis

❑ ***Review of market trends and technical analysis.*** Investor appetite for the type of paper and the impact of macro factors, such as equity markets and the strength of the economy

❑ ***Sector analysis of an issuer or borrower.*** Some basic questions are: what are the competitive forces and comparative advantages of the issuer? What kind of new technologies and products are developed?

❑ ***Financial analysis of an issuer or borrower.*** Review of the earnings, cash flow, and capital structure with a focus on liquidity, debt capacity, and refinancing risk

❑ ***Management analysis.*** Strategy, controls, depth of experience, track records, and incentives are reviewed, preferably including direct communication with management. Furthermore, we have to question the credit friendliness: is there an LBO, M&A risk; are there plans of dividend increases or share buybacks leading to a higher leverage?

Evaluation of the Issue

Having established a view on the company or borrower via the quantitative internal rating and the qualitative analysis, the specifics of the issue are evaluated. Important questions in this context are: Where is the instrument in the capital structure? Can structural subordination evolve or worsen over time? Are there specific covenants (like maximum leverage, change of control puts, or coupon step-ups)? What is or will be the precise reference entity for the CDS?

What is the relative value for the instrument? Are there further technical features like call options? Additionally, market-related matters must be considered such as supply and demand imbalances for particular securities and derivatives thereof.

External Research

The market provides plenty of research. The differentiating success factor is the ability to extrapolate ideas from a variety of sources. The choice of research provider will vary depending on their strength in particular areas.

❑ Rating agencies suffer from the reputation of generally lagging in rating changes. Nonetheless, their research and publications will affect the markets so they must factor into the analysis.

❑ Financial institutions are a valuable source of both equity and fixed-income company and technical information. However, the analysis must consider the potential positive outlook bias of *sell-side research*.

❑ Independent research houses add valuable, detailed bottom-up research for single credits including deep analysis of covenant language or possible structure subordination.

❑ Actuaries and accountancy firms form another vital source of information for the insurance sector (for example, the Financial Services Authority's [FSA] rollout of solvency rules for UK insurers).

❑ Industry and trade magazines are used selectively as a source of early signals and indicators of turning points in a sector's health.

Relative Value Opportunities

The internal evaluation of the company or borrower is then compared to the external opinions to determine the asset's risk versus reward profile and possible relative value opportunities. Relative value opportunities fall into four broad categories:

Issuer Specific

The internal analysis may result in a different view of an issuer's credit strength versus the market. This can be either stronger, which would suggest going long the issuer, or weaker, which would suggest shorting the issuer.

Intrasector

Pairs of issuers are identified that have similar characteristics and ratings but where the internal analysis indicates diverging credit trends.

Cross-Sector

This opportunity arises when two sectors with similar sensitivities or drivers show significantly abnormal credit spread differentials.

Capital Structure

This category includes anomalous valuation differentials between securities of the same issuer. These can be either two different debt issues or debt versus equity.

Strategies

This section describes the primary strategies of the multistrategy credit hedge fund shown in **FIGURE 1.1**. While these strategies vary in structure and approach, they share the credit analysis process described previously as a common foundation.

Strategy 1: Corporates Selection—Select Winners

The objective of this strategy is to structure a diversified portfolio of credits, which we expect to outperform the market, while ensuring that a

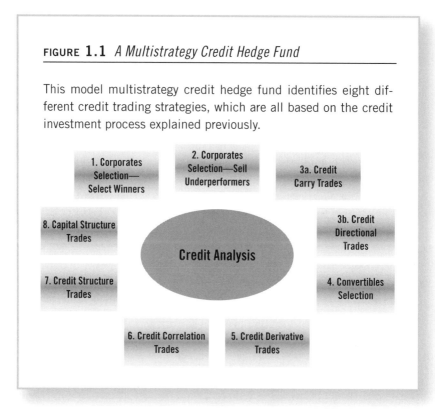

FIGURE **1.1** *A Multistrategy Credit Hedge Fund*

This model multistrategy credit hedge fund identifies eight different credit trading strategies, which are all based on the credit investment process explained previously.

substantial portion of the systemic market risk (beta) has been hedged, thus, generating excess returns (alpha).

Constructing the Portfolio

The portfolio is created by purchasing approximately thirty corporate bonds (fifteen minimum), which are expected to outperform the market (that is, their current credit spreads are high relative to the risks as determined by the internal analysis). When selecting these bonds, spread duration is important as it defines the bond's sensitivity to spread movements. This sensitivity (the bond's mark-to-market risk) increases with duration. The spread carry is compared to the mark-to-market risk to determine a break-even spread. The break-even spread is the maximum spread widening that can be absorbed from the instrument's spread income before the bond underperforms versus a government bond with similar maturity. As compared to investment grade corporate bonds, high-yield and crossover bonds with short maturities and relatively high spread incomes may provide a more favorable carry to mark-to-market risk ratio.

Hedge the Currency and Interest-Rate Risk

Any currency exposure within a bond is hedged into base currency. Rather than hedge the interest-rate risk of each individual bond in the portfolio, an efficient solution is to use macro swaps where the notional amounts of four or five swap maturities are selected to protect the bond portfolio not only from parallel yield curve shifts but also potential yield curve twists. Liquid government bonds can be used to adjust the hedge on an ongoing basis (for example, for small amounts of new issues, however, this technique entails basis risk).

Hedge the Market Credit Risk

Going short an index (that is, buying credit default protection) is an effective method for hedging the market credit risk of the portfolio. There are several indexes available. Ideally, the credit spread duration of the index used should match that of the position or (sub-) portfolio. The iTraxx five- and ten-year indexes are the core hedge instruments of choice as they are more liquid and less expensive to trade. To the extent that these hedges are imperfect, biases in the corporate bonds versus credit index residual risks (basis risk) should be monitored and any overweighting in a sector (for example, telecom, or individual corporate with a higher beta) can be identified, and if undesired, hedged by using subindexes or high-volatility or crossover indexes. Insofar as credit indexes tend to be more liquid than individual credits, a lag effect (or skew) can occur, leading to temporary imprecise hedges and short-term mark-to-market risks.

Result

Following this approach, the portfolio should be hedged against currency risk, most interest-rate risk, and the majority of the market credit risk. The residual risks retained within the portfolio are predominantly the pure idiosyncratic credit risks of individual issuers, which are the key drivers of this strategy.

This is an ongoing strategy with expected annual turnover of 200%. All the components and risk dimensions of this position should be measured and marked-to-market, and the position evaluated on at least a daily basis as described more fully in the portfolio risk management process section in Chapter 6.

Strategy 2: Corporates Selection—Sell Underperformers

This strategy is essentially the opposite of Strategy 1. In this strategy, credits with the worst expected returns are selected and sold short. However, shorting corporate bonds entails additional risks as borrowing may be difficult and early repo calls or redemptions of the specific instrument can lead to significant squeezes resulting in price jumps and significant losses. These additional risks can deny the portfolio manager the time necessary to wait for his fundamental expectation to materialize and realize the profit in the trade. Therefore, the instrument of choice for shorting credits is a credit default swap. Insofar as credit default swaps are a pure credit instrument, there is no need to hedge interest-rate risk. As with Strategy 1, credit market risk should be hedged with liquid credit indexes like iTraxx. However, in this case, the indexes should be bought (that is, sell credit default protection). In addition to hedging the market credit risk, buying the index or selling credit default protection also generates positive cash flow to offset the carry costs of shorting the credits.

Similar to Strategy 1, select winners, Strategy 2, sell underperformers, is an ongoing strategy.

Strategy 3: Credit Pair Trades

The objective of this strategy is to exploit spread differentials between two credit instruments. The execution of this strategy centers on investing in long or short credit pairs using corporate bonds, credit default swaps, credit indexes, and other credit instruments and derivatives. Generally, each of the two instruments is from different issuers. However, these trades can be established between two instruments from the same issuer to exploit views about the issuer's credit curve or the pricing relationship of the different instruments.

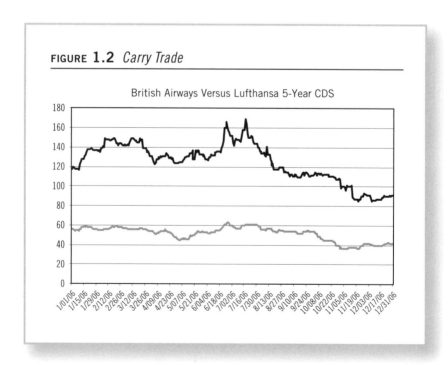

FIGURE 1.2 *Carry Trade*

British Airways Versus Lufthansa 5-Year CDS

There are two varieties of pair trades determined by the expectation of the spread: (3a) credit carry trades assume that the spread will remain relatively stable, and (3b) directional spread trades assume spreads will change.

Strategy 3a: Credit Carry Trades

There are two ways to execute credit carry trades: (1) buying a higher yielding corporate bond or selling protection via a credit default swap and (2) selling (shorting) lower yielding corporate bonds or buying protection via a credit default swap where the expectation is that the spread between the two will remain relatively stable, thus, earning a positive carry. To reduce systemic risk, the issuers should be from the same sector.

In this example (**FIGURE 1.2**) of long British Airways versus short Lufthansa, both five-year CDS, an intrasector credit pair was found where we assumed a stable spread differential. The biggest downside risk of this trade is that British Airways defaults. Additionally, there is the risk of negative mark-to-market if British Airways's spread widens more than Lufthansa's. In the no-default case, a permanent income of 61 bps (117 versus 56 at beginning of 2006) will be realized from the spread differential. Additionally, if British Airways's spread tightens more than Lufthansa's, positive mark-to-market will be generated, which would likely result in profit taking from an early unwind of the trade.

Carry trades have an average holding period of six months.

Strategy 3b: Credit Directional Trades

There are two ways to execute credit directional trades: (1) buying a corporate bond or selling credit default swap protection where the spread is expected to tighten relative to the second instrument and (2) selling a corporate bond or buying protection via a credit default swap on a second issuer where the spread is expected to widen relative to the first instrument. Profit will be realized when the spreads move in the expected directions, and the positions are unwound.

In this example (**FIGURE 1.3**) of a trade involving Fiat versus Valeo, the expectation was that Fiat can manage the turnaround within a difficult industry by strict financial discipline, improving operating efficiency and developing attractive new models. Valeo might potentially be prone to leveraged buyout (LBO) risk, which in this case will lead to a substantial spread widening. Besides the significant profit from the spread tightening of the long leg, the spread differential generated positive carry. These trades are easy to execute, as they require almost no interest-rate and currency hedging. Investing in this strategy is a relatively easy way to increase the fund's leverage.

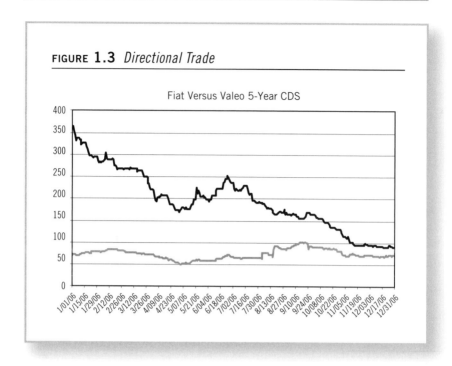

FIGURE 1.3 *Directional Trade*

Fiat Versus Valeo 5-Year CDS

Strategy 4: Convertibles Selection

The special feature of convertible bonds is the opportunity to gain exposure to equity movements and volatility while benefiting from the instrument's convexity. The convertible market is characterized by some inefficiencies: the value of the convertible sometimes does not properly reflect the value of its individual components (bond floor and equity call option). This is especially true for new issues. Nevertheless, secondary trading can also be profitable and is essential to maintain good relationships in order to receive an allocation of attractive new issues.

Insofar as the credit fund maintains long positions in convertibles, the objective of this strategy is to identify convertibles whose price undervalues its components. This is achieved through an analysis process specific to convertible bonds and will include credit (that is, bond) analysis, equity and equity volatility forecasts, and analysis of any other relevant embedded options. See **FIGURE 1.4**.

The first step is to analyze the bond, which forms the floor of the convertible's value. The bond component of a convertible bond is essentially equal to a corporate bond. Therefore, there is substantial overlap in the investment process with that of a regular corporate bond. However, subordinations and optionalities occur more frequently in convertible bonds as compared to corporate bonds and, therefore, must be carefully assessed.

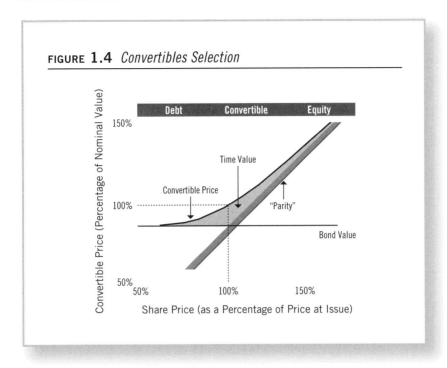

FIGURE **1.4** *Convertibles Selection*

The second step is to analyze and forecast the underlying equity. As compared to a credit analysis, which is concerned with downside risk and its protection, the analysis of the equity component is more concerned with growth and upside potential. This difference in perspective may result in bondholder versus shareholder conflicts demanding a careful fundamental bottom-line judgment of the entire complex convertible.

The third step is the valuation of the embedded equity call option, especially the implied volatility, and considering all the option *Greeks*: delta, gamma, vega, theta, and so on.

The fourth step is to evaluate any other options embedded in the convertible bond.

The result of this thorough analysis is a risk versus return assessment based on a total return forecast for all the relevant components. Having identified an undervaluation, or expecting an outperformance of the equity versus the equity index, the convertible bond is purchased. Undesired risks, such as currency, interest rate, or equity may be minimized or eliminated through hedging.

Recently, convertible bonds in general have performed well given the strong equity market returns and the limited supply of new attractive convertible bond issues.

Strategy 5: Credit Derivatives Trades

A high level of product innovation characterizes credit derivatives. There is a wide range of instruments like financial sector subindex or options on credit indexes. Successful managers embrace the innovation and position themselves to exploit new products and strategies as they are fully understood within the context of the investment process and can be precisely captured in the risk management process explained in Chapter 6.

For example, credit futures and options can be used to invest directly in directional spread movements or to construct trading strategies, such as straddles, to exploit credit volatility views. Unfortunately, the transaction costs are still high but are expected to come down in the near future.

Index and subindex products might be used to efficiently establish strategies similar to the single-name strategies discussed earlier.

Strategy 6: Credit Correlation Trades

The objective of this strategy is to forecast the correlation among credits and structure appropriate trades using collateralized debt obligation (CDO) tranches. For example, an expected increase in correlation will create an opportunity to sell protection on a CDO equity tranche and buy

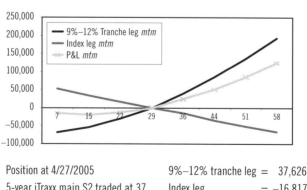

FIGURE 1.5 *Credit Correlation Trade*

- Buy EUR10 M protection on 5-year iTraxx 9%–12% S2 tranche at 14.5 bps
- Sell protection on EUR5 M of 5-year iTraxx main S2 at 28 bps
- Carry neutral, positive convexity, credit short and long correlation

Legend:
— 9%–12% Tranche leg *mtm*
— Index leg *mtm*
✕ P&L *mtm*

Position at 4/27/2005	9%–12% tranche leg =	37,626
5-year iTraxx main S2 traded at 37	Index leg =	−16,817
	Net P&L =	**+20,809**
	Trade DV01 =	**+2,750**

protection on a senior tranche of the same underlying pool. (Refer to later chapters for a detailed discussion of the mechanics of CDOs and indexes and the key concepts underlying this trade.) The manager primarily uses liquid iTraxx tranches to minimize transaction costs and to increase liquidity and data quality. See **FIGURE 1.5**.

In addition to strategies based on a directional view of credit correlation, tranches can be used to construct a positive convexity position.

The objective of this trade is to establish *disaster insurance* where the strategy performs especially well in a sharply widening spread environment while restricting losses in a substantial spread-tightening environment. Achieving this asymmetric profile requires convexity. An underlying assumption of this trade is that an environment of sharply increasing spreads will exhibit an increase in the correlation among the credits and vice versa. Here, protection was purchased on the 9% to 12% mezzanine tranche. Protection was sold on the main iTraxx index to generate premium income to offset the majority of premium paid and establish a carry neutral profile. The net position was long correlation (that is, profits increase as correlation increases) with the desired positive convexity (the profit increase is greater than the loss for a given amount of change in the correlation) while paying very little net carry.

To reduce the mark-to-market risk of this pair trade, the delta between the mezzanine tranche and the main tranche must be carefully constructed and monitored on an ongoing basis. In early May 2005, a serious correlation breakdown occurred in which the mezzanine tranches had an almost disastrous performance. This breakdown in the expected correlation relationships resulted in unreliable deltas and insufficient hedges. The full extent of the possible downside risk of long correlation exposure was painfully illustrated as major market players (structured credit hedge funds and proprietary trading desks) experienced heavy losses.

Credit correlation trades have an average holding period of three months, but the disaster insurance trade explained here is a rather long-horizon, structural portfolio position.

Strategy 7: Credit Structure Strategies

The objective of this strategy is to earn additional yield by investing in attractive credit structures. The classic example of this type of trade is to invest in (that is, sell protection on) a first-to-default (FTD) credit basket and short (that is, buy protection) on the individual names within the basket. (Refer to Chapter 2 for a discussion of the mechanics and key principles underlying FTD basket options and swaps.)

In this trade, protection is sold on a $5 million FTD basket consisting of seven issuers. This trade is leveraged in that it is exposed to each of the

FIGURE 1.6 *Credit Structures*

Trade P&L—Broad Spread Move Scenario

- Sell 5 M protection in FTD basket (seven names) and buy protection on individual names.
- This trade is delta neutral, positive carry (160 bps), positive convexity, long default and long correlation exposure.
- The structure benefits from general spread movements but is long idiosyncratic risk. Single-name idiosyncratic risk is dynamically hedged.

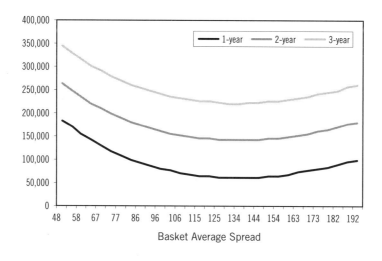

seven names for $5 million (but only to the first one to default). Each of the individual seven issuers is actively partially (that is, delta) hedged by buying protection via CDSs. The hedge ratios used are a function of the assessment regarding the probability of default of each of the individual issuers in the basket and the correlation among them.

This trade generates positive carry. **FIGURE 1.6** illustrates the estimated trade profit and loss over one-, two-, and three-year time horizons. A tightening of credit spreads (that is, a reduction in the basket's average spread) should increase the value of the sold protection in the basket more than the offsetting reduction in the value of the credit protection bought on the individual issuers within the basket. Effective delta hedging could result in an increase in the net value of the position in an increasing spread environment as well.

FIGURE **1.7** *Delta Hedges*

04/27/2005	POSITION	NOTIONAL	*MTM*	DV01
FTD basket	sell protection	5,000,000	−111,946	−8,526
RSA	buy protection	2,400,000	−3,706	1,147
TUI	buy protection	2,750,000	18,117	1,262
EAUG	buy protection	2,000,000	9,866	947
EIRCOM	buy protection	2,600,000	23,613	1,207
AHOLD	buy protection	2,500,000	16,599	1,162
THYSSEN	buy protection	2,150,000	30,007	999
DCX	buy protection	2,200,000	53,020	1,000
DCX	buy protection	500,000	2,284	231
Net P&PL			**37,855**	**−571**

The parallel upward shifts in the curves over the years are a reflection of the increased value of the spread annuity over longer time horizons.

However, this is not a riskless trade. The positive spread carry must compensate for the risk of the correlation assumption being incorrect (the trade is long correlation) and the *jump-to-default risk* (the trade is long default risk). The models used to evaluate basket transactions assume *orderly defaults*: the weakest credit (that is, the credit with the highest spread) defaults first, and the credit deteriorates in an orderly manner before defaulting. Jump-to-default risk is the risk that a credit other than the credit with the highest spread is the first to default, and it does so without first showing deterioration in the spread. This is a concern because delta hedging is partial hedging and its effectiveness is predicated on continually adjusting the hedge ratio. As a credit within a basket deteriorates, the delta hedge ratios would change and would shift more protection against the deteriorating credit. The goal is to fully hedge the deteriorating credit by the time it defaults. If the credit jumps to default (that is, there is no orderly deterioration), the risk manager will not have adjusted the hedge ratio appropriately, and the defaulted credit will not be fully covered, resulting in a loss.

Accordingly, this trade requires an effective assessment of the residual risks versus the positive carry. An example of this active adjustment can be seen in **FIGURE 1.7** where two positions for DCX (DaimlerChrysler) are listed. We bought further €500,000 notional protection to increase the hedge as we assumed a short-term weakening of the issuer's credit profile.

Credit structure trades have an average holding period of three months.

Strategy 8: Capital Structure Trades

The objective of this strategy is to generate positive returns by identifying and exploiting debt to equity relative value trades. This category also includes various permutations of capital arbitrage structures, especially finding debt equity trades within a company.

Important triggers are shifts from bondholder value to shareholder value and vice versa. An example of the first scenario is ISS. In March 2005 ISS became an LBO target and a substantial increase in leverage occurred leading to an instantaneously massive credit spread widening (five-year CDS widened 250 bps). On the other hand, ISS shareholders gained, as a premium of 30% was offered to purchase outstanding equity. The trade of choice was to buy protection on ISS credit and go long ISS shares or equity options. These events are, in general, difficult to foresee, but the potential trading profits are substantial. In our opinion, speaking to senior management can give some flavor about potential relative biases and future dynamics between bondholder and shareholder value. It makes it easier to assess possible important corporate actions, such as debt-financed acquisitions, and share buybacks, which can then lead to spotting attractive debt to equity trades.

To establish the appropriate hedge ratios, it is essential to make recovery assumptions and compare implied volatilities for every element of an entity's capital structure in order to identify the most efficient instruments and most profitable investment opportunities.

Chapter Notes

1. Anthony Saunders and Linda Allen. 2002. *Credit Risk Measurement*, 2nd ed. New York: John Wiley & Sons.

2. A thorough description of discriminant analysis is beyond the scope of this chapter. A more detailed description of the technique can be found in many advanced-level statistics textbooks. A seminal research using discriminant analysis to assess credit quality is Edward Altman's article, "Financial Ratios, Discriminant

Analysis and the Prediction of Corporate Bankruptcy," *Journal of Finance* 23 (1968): 589–609.

3. For major parts of our qualitative analysis in this section, we use Michael E. Porter's concepts as described in his books *Competitive Strategy* (New York: Free Press, 1980) and *Competitive Advantage* (New York: Free Press, 1985).

CHAPTER 2

Distressed Debt Strategies

STEVEN D. PERSKY

D istressed investing is an investment strategy that is inherently op- portunistic. Distress is an unstable characteristic. Companies, industries, and countries generally do not remain distressed for long periods of time. Typically, a series of circumstances will combine to cause distress, and over time the problems are addressed and resolved so that the distressed entity either liquidates or recovers. Consequently, dis- tressed investors need to adapt to changing circumstances so that they can profit from new distressed opportunities as they occur.

The most lucrative distressed opportunities arise when, prior to the distressed event, there has never been a high yield/distressed market for the assets that have become distressed. Asian distressed debt was a very good example of such an opportunity. Prior to the Asian crisis, which began in 1997, there was very little high yield or distressed Asian debt. An Asian investment bank, Peregrine, had begun to develop a high-yield Asian debt market, but it was still quite nascent; and the firm collapsed in early 1998, an early casualty of the Asian debt crisis. Most Asian debt was issued as investment-grade debt at a spread to U.S. Treasuries. Investors were largely financial institutions that were restricted to investing in investment-grade debt.

When the Asian crisis began, much of the non-Japanese Asian debt was downgraded to below investment grade. The ratings decline and sharply reduced risk appetite among Asian investors caused a large in- crease in the supply of Asian debt. However, there was very little de- mand. The early investors in Asian debt had been badly burned by the decline in the value of their holdings and so were unable to absorb additional supply.

High-yield and distressed investors were unfamiliar with Asia and understandably leery about bankruptcy laws and regulations in countries like Indonesia, the Philippines, and Thailand. In fact, most distressed and high-yield investors restrict their investments to G7 countries. Other concerns were currency exchange rates, which were quite volatile during the period. Consequently, the downgraded Asian debt was sold into a vacuum. Prices collapsed and the market became illiquid with a preponderance of sellers and very few buyers. Prices fell to levels that looked very cheap based on the metric of EBITDA/interest coverage or debt to EBITDA.

Gradually, more adventurous capital was attracted to the high potential returns of distressed Asian debt. These early investors were generally opportunistic distressed investors: hedge funds and proprietary desks of investment banks, which act like hedge funds. These investors had not had exposure to Asian debt as it was too "high quality" and so had not taken losses. They had risk appetite and were able to approach the opportunity without the baggage of Asian institutions, which were struggling to stay afloat during the crisis.

A number of hedge fund advisers established dedicated Asian funds to take advantage of the situation, including the Avenue Asia Fund, Montpelier Asia Recovery Fund, and others. Salomon Brothers, UBS, and other investment banks allocated capital and people to exploit the opportunity. As capital began to flow to distressed Asian debt, prices began to stabilize and liquidity increased.

At the same time, the macroeconomic environment in Asia began to improve. A major element of the crisis was crushing devaluations of currencies that had been pegged to the U.S. dollar. These included the Thai baht, Philippine peso, and Indonesian rupiah. These currencies fell to as little as one-eighth of their pegged value versus the dollar.

The devaluations were a major cause of corporate distress as Asian companies saw their dollar-denominated liabilities balloon. But at the same time, the devaluations caused a huge decline in imports and an enormously improved export environment. Countries that had been running large current account deficits saw these deficits rapidly turn into surpluses.

As the current account situation improved, currencies stabilized. Stabilizing currencies allowed governments to lower interest rates, which helped economic recovery. A virtuous cycle began of stabilizing currencies, falling interest rates, and improved economic performance.

As the macroeconomic situation improved, prices began to rise, which attracted more capital from existing investors and new investors. The improving macroeconomic situation also encouraged the Asian corporate debtors to focus on debt restructurings. Their thinking was that they wanted to restructure before the currencies and corporate performance improved more and gave investors higher recovery expectations.

Astra International was an example of a distressed Asian corporation with bank debt, public debt, and equity outstanding. Astra was one of the largest companies in Indonesia. Its businesses included automobile and motorcycle manufacturing and distribution, telecom, palm oil, and other operations. When the Indonesian rupiah devalued from roughly 2,500 IDR/USD to over 16,000 IDR/USD in early 1998, Astra's liabilities, which were mostly denominated in U.S. dollars, multiplied sevenfold. At the same time, the economic crisis collapsed demand for new automobiles and motorcycles, the company's core business. Astra chose to restructure its debt into three tranches of debt, which would amortize successively. The coupons were lowered and once the restructuring was complete, Astra began making interest payments on its restructured debt.

Investors were willing to take a fairly hefty haircut in order to induce Astra to become current on the restructured debt. Astra also lowered the coupon rate on the restructured debt. The combination of a reduced face amount of debt and lower coupons sharply reduced the interest burden of Astra.

As currencies stabilized and Asian economies began to recover, prices of Asian debt began to rise. It is interesting to note that in September 2001, prices of many Indonesian corporations performed quite strongly. This outperformance during that crisis month illustrates how distressed situations can act independently of major markets, as performance becomes much more tied to the underlying credit fundamentals of the distressed entity.

A second example of a profitable distressed opportunity was the crisis that befell high-yield collateralized bond obligations (CBO) beginning in 2002. CBO are asset-backed securities where the underlying collateral is high-yield bonds. Most CBO were issued as investment-grade debt to investment-grade issuers. The CBO were structured so that the senior tranches received investment-grade ratings based on the subordination of the equity tranche. The equity tranche was typically unrated and was often retained by the issuer or manager. The attraction for investment grade investors was that the investment-grade-rated senior debt was typically cheaper than similarly rated corporate debt.

Initially, the CBO market was exclusively an investment-grade market. The securities were not very liquid, and there was not a lot of secondary trading. Investors were content to clip their coupons, and the market began to grow as high-yield CBO became more accepted. Corporate default rates remained quite low in 1998 through 1999 but began to trend up sharply in 2000, and default levels set records in 2001 and 2002. As a result of defaults in the bonds owned in the CBO structures, many CBO were downgraded as well.

When CBO began to suffer downgrades below investment grade, many of the investment-grade investors were forced to sell their CBO holdings. The problem was that traditional high-yield and distressed investors were unfamiliar with CBO as there had never been a high-yield CBO market. In addition, CBO analysis requires systems to analyze the underlying assets and predict future cash flows based on assumptions of credit defaults and prepayments. High-yield investors did not have this technology and so were unable to analyze the complicated structured CBO.

As default rates moved up in 2001 and 2002, high-yield CBO became distressed. Prices of many CBO were trading at 20% discounts to the value of the underlying collateral. In other words, there was an arbitrage available of purchasing the CBO and selling short the underlying securities to achieve a riskless return. This discount was available because the supply of downgraded CBO had overwhelmed the potential investor base.

As hedge funds and other intrepid investors began to become familiar with these securities, demand began to grow. Many distressed debt investors began to build large positions of CBO, and some established dedicated funds to exploit the opportunity. Gradually, CBO prices stabilized and liquidity began to return to the market. CBO discounts began to narrow as competition for these securities began to grow. Over time, the discount available almost disappeared.

The BEA 1998-1A A2A is a good example of what befell high-yield CBO. The security was issued in May 1998 at a spread of 85 bps over swaps. This was the second and largest tranche of a high-yield CBO, which was issued by Bear Stearns and managed by BEA Associates, a well-known, high-yield manager. At issuance in May 1998, the A2A tranche was rated AAA by both Fitch and S&P. As default rates rose in 2001, the bonds were downgraded to BBB by S&P and Moody's, which was now rating the bond. Fitch did not downgrade the bond to BBB until 2002. In 2002, both major rating agencies downgraded the bond to junk. At this point, many investment-grade investors were forced to sell the security because of its downgrade. However, the high-yield market was in disarray and unfamiliarity with CBO structures further hampered liquidity.

At the end of 2002, the A1 security, which was to be paid off prior to amortization of the A2A, was fully paid off, and so the A2A became the next security to receive payment of interest and principal. Despite the likelihood of immediate payments of cash flow, the A2A was trading at a large discount to net asset value (NAV). This discount was close to 20% during the early part of 2003. It is interesting to note that because of rapid amortization, 61% of the principal of this security was repaid by the end of December 2004. So investors who purchased this security at a large discount to NAV captured 60% of that discount in less than two years.

Most traditional distressed investors restrict their efforts to the United States and perhaps a few more of the G7 countries. They argue, correctly, that in most countries, bankruptcy laws are nonexistent, untested, or unreliable. Consequently, they avoid examining any opportunities that arise outside of their preferred environment. As a result, securities of distressed companies in developing countries or even in countries such as France can become very cheap relative to the underlying value, as there are few investors willing to invest.

One way to separate countries in terms of their bankruptcy laws is to view countries that derive their bankruptcy laws from England. In addition to the United Kingdom, these include the United States, Canada, Australia, New Zealand, Hong Kong, Japan, Singapore, Bermuda, and Grand Cayman. In these countries, investors can have a high degree of confidence that they will be able to rely on bankruptcy laws and enforce their rights. In other countries, investors can take a conservative approach and assume that borrowers will not repay their debts unless they have a compelling reason to do so, as the investors will be unable to rely on the courts to enforce their rights.

Often, borrowers will have compelling business reasons to restructure their debt. One example was an Argentine company called Industrias Metalurgicas Pescarmona SA (IMPSA). IMPSA is an engineering and construction company specializing in building power projects. Like most Argentine companies, much of its debt was dollar denominated and when Argentina defaulted and the Argentina peso devalued in early 2002, its liabilities ballooned at the same time that its domestic business prospects cratered. Most Argentine corporations followed the sovereign's example and stopped paying interest or principal when due, and prices of Argentine corporate and sovereign paper fell into the twenties.

IMPSA, however, had new business prospects outside of Argentina but knew that it would be unlikely to be awarded new contracts if it was in bankruptcy—hence, its compelling reason to restructure quickly. IMPSA offered to exchange its issue of 9.25% due May 2002, for new debt that would mature in 2011. The new debt would not pay interest until May 2003, and then the coupon would increase to 5.75% until May 2006 when the coupon would increase once more to 8.75%. IMPSA told its investors that new contracts would begin to generate cash flow that would allow it to service its debt, and so bondholders agreed to restructure the debt without a principal haircut but with a below-market coupon and an extended amortization schedule. As a result of IMPSA's aggressive steps to restructure, it earned the distinction of being the first Argentine company to restructure its debt.

If companies reside in countries where bankruptcy laws are unreliable and they do not have a compelling reason to restructure, it can often be impossible to force a restructuring or gain control of the company's property. One example was C&P Homes (C&P), a Philippine corporate property developer of low-end housing. The company owned a substantial amount of land around Manila and had issued dollar-denominated debt to finance its land purchases and to develop the land. However, when the Asia crisis occurred, land values collapsed and the company ran out of cash. The company suggested a restructuring under which creditors would have taken a large haircut. Creditors explored legal avenues to foreclose on C&P's holdings. However, despite spending substantial time and legal fees on these efforts, creditors were unable to gain control of company property or force liquidation because of the lack of reliable bankruptcy laws in the Philippines. C&P's controlling shareholder was Senator Manuel Villar who was able to use his position to further stymie creditor efforts to force a restructuring or foreclose on C&P property. It was an example of the downside of investing in corporations in countries without reliable bankruptcy laws. Creditors were powerless to enforce their rights and were left with nearly valueless securities.

Early distressed investors focused exclusively on finding undervalued assets to purchase, and many have generated attractive returns by relying on long-only strategies. However, long-only investors forgo the opportunity to use their credit skills to make money on short opportunities, and they also expose their portfolios to substantial mark-to-market losses should credit and equity markets decline sharply.

Most professional investors agree that short-selling is more difficult than investing from the long side. Some go further and opine that the mark of a truly exceptional hedge fund manager is one who can profit on the short side. It is not intuitively clear why it is more difficult to make money on the short side apart from the fact that financial markets tend to have positive returns over time and so long-side players, on average, have the wind at their back while the wind is in the face of short sellers. One hurdle faced by short sellers and not encountered by long players is securing a borrow. In order to short shares of stock or bonds, a short-seller must first secure the borrow of these securities and feel a high level of confidence that the borrow will not be recalled in the near term.

The smaller the issue of securities to be shorted, the more difficult to secure the borrow. Once a company announces significant problems, short sellers rush to short their securities, and it may become difficult to borrow their shares. For example, it was very difficult to borrow debt issued by the network airline carriers including, American Airlines, Northwest Airlines, and Delta during the first four months of 2005 as these were heavily shorted.

The growth of credit derivatives has greatly eased the borrowing constraint. When entering into a credit derivative trade, there is no need to deliver the security and hence no need to be able to borrow the security. So investors wishing to short airline debt can enter into trades in which they are purchasing credit default insurance. This type of transaction allows them to achieve a short position in airline debt. Billions of dollars of notional amount of credit default trades have been transacted, and a large part of the popularity of this type of security is the solution it provides to the problem of borrowing securities to sell short.

Recently, some investment banks have begun entering into credit default trades on mezzanine tranches of subprime home equity loans. The mezzanine tranches tend to be relatively small (typically less than $50MM) and so effectively impossible to borrow and short. However, the credit default trades solve the borrowing problem. Recent trades include the Novastar Home Equity Loan 2004-4 B3 tranche rated Baa3/BBB. This tranche is $25MM and so would be impossible to short without the use of a derivative transaction.

Although credit default swaps do not require delivery of securities at the initiation of the trade, in the event of a default, the settlement process generally requires the purchaser of default insurance to deliver the referenced security to the seller of default insurance within a very brief time frame. Consequently, after some recent bankruptcy announcements, some of the defaulted securities have appreciated sharply as long default insurance players rush to purchase the securities. In April 2005 just before Eagle Picher, Inc. filed for bankruptcy, its 9.75% bond maturing 9/1/13 was trading at 55%. After it filed for bankruptcy, the security briefly rose to seventy-one before falling back into the mid-sixties. It seemed clear that much of its rapid appreciation postbankruptcy was caused by owners of default insurance rushing to purchase the security so that they could deliver it to the seller of the default insurance.

CHAPTER 3

Four Synthetic CDO Trading Strategies

ANDREA PETRELLI, JUN ZHANG,

SANTA FEDERICO, AND VIVEK KAPOOR

A common market standard has evolved for the pricing of synthetic CDOs, as described in Chapter 10. This has been the subject of much research and discussion. Less understood are the risk-reward profiles of popular CDO trading strategies and the associated capitalization requirements. Indeed, there is no commonly agreed risk and capital model for even the index product tranches. There are two main reasons for this state of affairs:

1 The popular techniques for pricing CDO tranches have not directly addressed replication and hedging errors (accounting for spread diffusion, spread jumps, and jumps to default with uncertain recovery) and, therefore, have not resulted in a commensurate maturing of the hedging and risk management paradigm.

2 The nonlinearity (relative to the reference asset performance) created by tranching renders ineffective and misleading the risk-aggregation methods that are based merely on marginal and linear spread sensitivity. These traditional risk aggregation methods continue to thrive in many risk management circles that have not effectively adapted to the revolution of structured credit products.

In practice, the task of risk assessment and developing a hedging strategy involves analyzing each of the variables that pricing models depend upon and developing a probabilistic description of the P&L associated with each trading strategy.

In this chapter, we will assess the credit-related risks in some popular synthetic CDO strategies. The risks in one elementary long-only credit trade (sell protection on a credit index) and three popular synthetic CDO strategies are compared. The CDO pricing model employed here to illustrate risk sensitivities is described in Chapter 10.

In particular, we compare the carry at inception with the downside risks of these trades. We illustrate how marginal spread and default sensitivities, which provide a good description for elementary credit strategies, are inadequate for more complex nonlinear CDO strategies. For each strategy, the spread and value on default sensitivities are shown, along with a comparison of the carry and value on default probability distributions.

After analyzing the risk characteristics of static portfolios in terms of default, spread, and correlation, we provide an exposition of dynamic hedging and risks. Specifically, we explore the equity trade (sell equity protection and buy index protection) and show how the trading P&L evolves and can be attributed to the different market variables.

Elementary Portfolio

Selling protection on an index of CDS is an example of an elementary credit portfolio, as depicted in **FIGURE 3.1**. The North American Investment Grade Index (CDX.NA.IG) consists of 125 credits, as described in Chapter 5. This index will be used to provide example calculations, and the risk profile for the CDO trades will be compared with risks incurred in simply selling protection on the index.

FIGURE 3.1 *Long Credit Index*

An elementary portfolio credit trade of selling protection on a pool of CDS. The premium cash-flow stream is denoted by the solid line, and the default contingent cash flows are denoted by the dotted line.

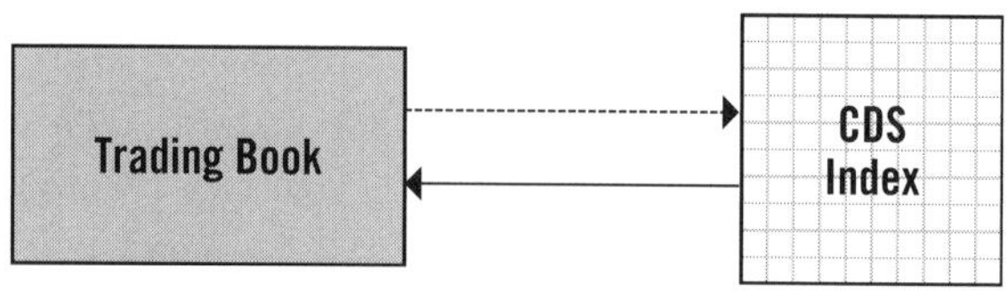

CDO Portfolios

Quotes on tranches referencing credit indexes and market participants' estimates of associated index deltas (CS01 hedge) are widely available on at least a daily frequency (for example, **TABLE 3.1**). These quotes sometimes are based on delta exchanges, which are ostensibly CS01 "hedges" for the tranches, which can, in certain strategies, be the long credit-risk driver. We focus on three CDO trades based on such an indexed product:

1 *Positive carry equity tranche trade.* Sell protection on the 0% to 3% tranche referencing the CDX.NA.IG index, and hedge CS01 exposure by buying protection on the index (**FIGURE 3.2**).

2 *Positive carry straddle trade.* Sell protection on 0% to 3% of the CDX.NA.IG index and hedge CS01 exposure by buying protection on the 7% to 10% tranche (**FIGURE 3.3**).

3 *Positive carry senior/mezzanine tranche trade.* Buy protection on the 7% to 10% tranche of the CDX.NA.IG index and hedge CS01 exposure by selling protection on the index (**FIGURE 3.4**).

It is worth noting that for these trades, the premium received as a result of selling credit protection exceeds the premium paid to immunize small-scale spread movements. The carry for these trades can be found by adding the running coupon to the time decay of the trade's mark-to-market (or approximated by simply amortizing the up-front payment over the tranche duration). This is particularly important because traditional risk-management systems focused on vanilla credit can be all too easily circumvented by these strategies, and the associated positive carry of these

---

TABLE 3.1 *Quotes on CDX.NA.IG.4 for March 31, 2005*

CDX.NA.IG.4—6/20/10—Ref 49—Assumes Delta Exchange

TRANCHE	DESC	INDICATIVE BID	OFFER	CORR (MID)	DELTA	AXE (PROT)
0–3%	Equity	500+33.00%	500+34.00%	19%	17.0x	B/S
3–7%	BBB–	195	203	5%	7.0x	B/S
7–10%	AAA	61	67	16%	2.8x	B/S
10–15%	AAA+	23	27	21%	1.1x	B/S
15–30%	Super Sen.	8	12	32%	0.3x	B/S

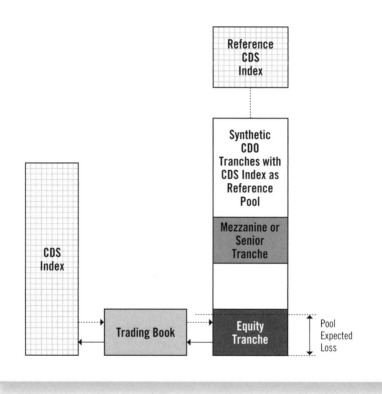

FIGURE 3.2 *Delta-Hedged Equity Tranche*

A popular CDO trade consists of selling protection on an equity tranche referencing a credit index, and purchasing protection on the credit index to hedge away to spot spread delta. The pool expected loss refers to the sum of the contingent legs of the CDS in the reference index (that is, it is the cost of buying default protection on the whole pool if the CDS contracts were all upfront pay).

Reference
CDS
Index

Synthetic
CDO
Tranches with
CDS Index as
Reference
Pool

Mezzanine or
Senior
Tranche

CDS
Index

Trading Book

Equity
Tranche

Pool
Expected
Loss

strategies makes them a popular choice. Why would anyone try to create positive cash flows with no delta exposure? Why not? Risk management functions are carefully monitoring delta exposures (that is, CS01, or "bond equivalent market values" as is customary in big bond shops). Risk capital has historically been proportional to credit delta exposure. Credit spread and default gamma/convexity (with respect to single name moves and market moves) and correlation risk measures do not exist in most risk-capital models.

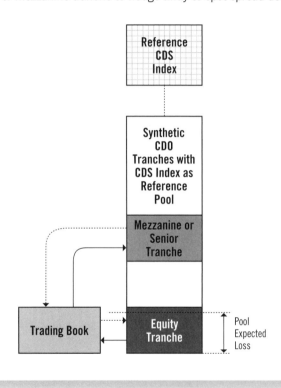

FIGURE **3.3** *Straddle*

Another popular CDO trade consists of selling protection on an equity tranche referencing a credit index and purchasing protection on a senior or mezzanine tranche to hedge away to spot spread delta.

Reference
CDS
Index

Synthetic
CDO
Tranches with
CDS Index as
Reference
Pool

Mezzanine or
Senior
Tranche

Trading Book

Equity
Tranche

Pool
Expected
Loss

Default

Marginal VOD

The change in mark-to-market value (*mtm*) due to an issuer spread widening unbounded is referred to as the value on default (VOD) to that issuer, as shown in **FIGURE 3.5**, which distinguishes reference entities by their five-year spread. For the long credit index trade, the sign of the VOD is negative: the spread on the index is the price of taking on default risk. The "delta-hedged" CDO trades also have negative marginal VODs to each reference entity in the pool. Within each positive-carry CDO strategy on CDX. NA.IG, the marginal VOD does not vary a great deal in this largely BBB pool. The marginal VODs for the different trading strategies are ordered by

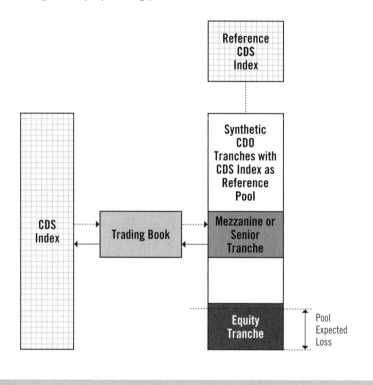

FIGURE 3.4 *Delta-Hedged Senior/Mezzanine Tranche*

In this CDO, trade protection is purchased on a senior or mezzanine tranche referencing a credit index, and the spot spread delta is hedged away by selling protection on the credit index.

the carry (at inception) of the strategy (that is, the greater the carry, the more negative is the marginal VOD). The carry associated with the formal "delta-hedged" CDO trade is clearly a compensation for taking on credit event risks. Whether the carry provides a trading book any excess spread over what is *fair* to take on credit risk is an interesting question. We will start to address that by comparing the default risk and carry of these strategies against the elementary credit strategy later. The carry for the straddle strategy is expressed in terms of the equity tranche notional in Figure 3.5.

Running VOD

By simultaneously defaulting multiple issuers, the *running* VOD of a trade can be found. As there are many possible 2-tuples, 3-tuples, and so on,

FIGURE **3.5** *Marginal Value on Default (VOD) Sensitivity for Three CDO Strategies and the Long Credit Index Trade.*

There are 125 issuers in the credit index and associated CDO analyzed here. The horizontal axis is the credit spread level of the distinct issuers, and the vertical axis is the marginal P&L impact of default (VOD) of distinct issuers.

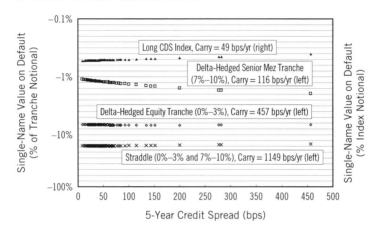

there is no unique running VOD, unless we are dealing with a homogeneous portfolio. The running VOD shown here is based on sorting the issuers in the order of decreasing spreads, and defaulting the top N names simultaneously. **FIGURES 3.6**, **3.7**, and **3.8** show the running VOD for the three different CDO strategies. All the strategies exhibit a "positive index gamma" type profile in the running VOD (that is, the losses due to a few defaults is less than the sum of the corresponding marginal VODs). All the strategies show a gain after the number of defaults exceeds a certain amount.

For the positive carry equity tranche trade or straddle, the concept of maximum loss is useful because there is a clearly defined maximum loss for any sequence of defaults (Figures 3.6 and 3.7). The concept becomes less clear for the positive carry senior/mezzanine tranche trade (Figure 3.8). After a certain number of defaults, the senior/mezzanine strategy shows a reversal of the P&L gains associated with an increasing number of defaults. This feature arises because after the CDO tranche is eaten through by defaults, there is no short exposure left. In general, the notion of a "maximum-loss" associated with a portfolio of CDO trades is not a viable

FIGURE **3.6** *Default Sensitivity of Delta-Hedged Equity Tranche (0% to 3%)*

The cumulative *mtm* impact due to defaults for the equity tranche strategy is shown here. The issuers are sorted by their five-year credit spread and the highest 1,2, ... N names are defaulted. The *mtm* changes can be decomposed into those arising from the CDO tranche and from the single name CDS. Due to upfront payments received for selling equity protection, the losses incurred due to defaults for the tranche level out at amounts less than the tranche notional. The CDS protection purchased via the index results in payoffs that grow linearly with the number of defaults. The net running default P&L impact is nonmonotonic, with the maximum loss scenario corresponding to five defaults (24% of equity tranche notional) and the breakeven scenario corresponding to eight defaults.

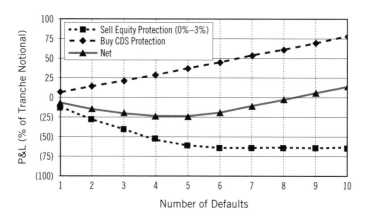

Source: CDX.NA.IG.4, March 31, 2005.

risk-management target because the maximum loss scenario can be wildly unrealistic (that is, all the names in the pool defaulting) and for a portfolio of trades the loss versus number of names defaulted can be highly irregular, depending on the names defaulted.

The positive-carry CDO trades tend to exhibit positive P&L under sufficiently large (or intermediately large) numbers of default within the pool. Therefore, for a portfolio of positive-carry CDO trades with non-overlapping pools, the most negative P&L associated with a small number of defaults will occur if those defaults occur in distinct pools.

Source: CDX.NA.IG.4, March 31, 2005.

FIGURE **3.7** *Default Sensitivity of Straddle (0% to 3% and 7% to 10% Tranche)*

The cumulative *mtm* impact due to defaults for the straddle strategy is shown here. The net running default P&L impact is nonmonotonic, with the maximum loss scenario corresponding to six defaults (47% of mezzanine tranche notional) and the breakeven scenario corresponding to ten defaults.

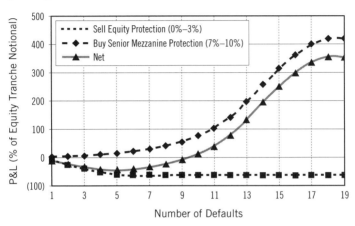

VOD Risk per Unit Carry

The next step beyond a running VOD assessment is to actually simulate default of the underlying issuers in a Monte Carlo (MC) setting, which generates many possible running VOD scenarios, and the associated *mtm* impact of defaults. Those MC *mtm* impact outcomes can be sorted, and the losses can be compared as multiples of the carry of the trades (for positive-carry trades). Such a measure is an important way to start comparing relative value, recognizing the residual VOD risks in the popular CDO trading strategies shown here. For the objective measure default simulation, one could employ Moody's KMV expected default frequency, Kamakura default probability, or empirical rating dependent default rates. A proprietary view on the issuer's balance sheets and default probabilities can also be taken in the specification of the issuer default probability.

Here, defaults are simulated using a normal copula with 25% asset correlation and Standard & Poor's 2004 corporate default table. The P&L impact of the issuers that default over a time horizon less than one year is found by repricing the portfolio under that scenario. This is repeated 50,000 times,

FIGURE **3.8** *Default Sensitivity of Delta-Hedged Senior Mezzanine Tranche (7% to 10%)*

The cumulative *mtm* impact due to defaults for the mezzanine tranche strategy is shown here. The net running default P&L impact is nonmonotonic, with the first maximum loss scenario (9% mezzanine tranche notional) corresponding to nine defaults, and the first breakeven scenario corresponding to eleven defaults.

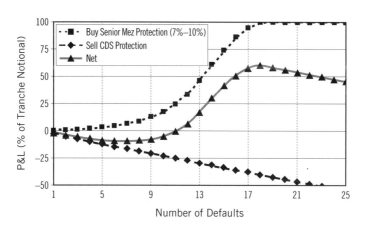

and the loss at different levels of confidence is shown in **FIGURE 3.9**. The losses are normalized by the annual cash flow associated with the different trades, to be able to compare the carry-default profile of the trades. The positive index gamma nature of the running VOD profile for the CDO strategies shows up as a relatively thin tail at high levels of confidence (that is, a linear long strategy encounters greater losses when the default rates are high, relative to long-short CDO strategies, for the same amount of initial carry). Such a view is quite different from simply looking at the absolute carry. For instance, the carry-default profiles of the different CDO strategies come out to be quite similar (on the specific date shown here), despite the absolute carry numbers being widely different. A proper risk-capital calculation based on default risk would render the carry per unit risk capital for these strategies to be quite similar. Also, at the 99% confidence level, the carry of the CDO strategies is not particularly attractive compared to a long credit index (on March 31, 2005). At higher confidence levels (for example, one-year S&P AA corporate default rate), the CDO strategies exhibit less default risk per unit carry compared to the long credit index strategy.

FIGURE **3.9** *One-Year Default Risk at Different Confidence Levels*

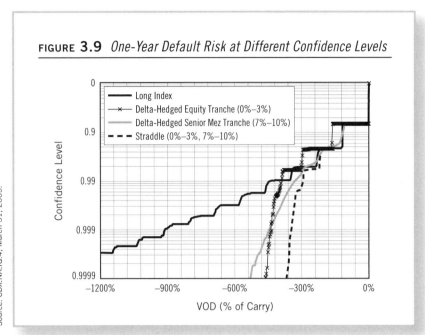

FIGURE **3.10** *Time History of Default Risk of the Positive Carry Equity CDO Strategy*

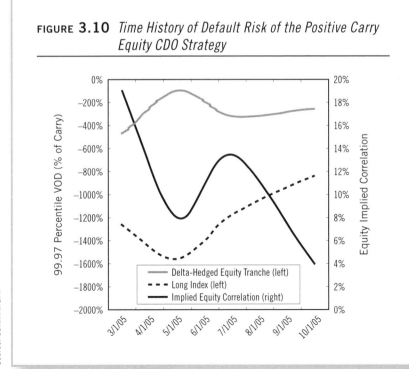

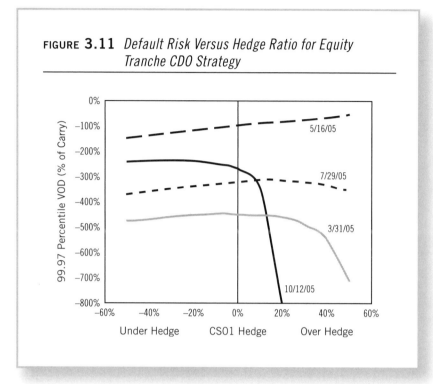

FIGURE 3.11 *Default Risk Versus Hedge Ratio for Equity Tranche CDO Strategy*

Source: CDX.NA.IG.4.

The observations made in Figure 3.9 are tied to the market data (issuer spreads, tranche pricing) and will change as the market spreads and pricing correlations change (**FIGURE 3.10**), as the credit-cycle evolves, and as market participants learn more about their risk-reward profiles. The residual VOD risk (expressed as a multiple of the trade carry) may be altered by hedging differently than an index-CS01 hedge. In some instances, buying more index protection for the equity trade reduces the VOD risk per unit carry (implying a cheap index protection and rich compensation for taking on equity tranche risk) and in other instances buying less protection reduces the VOD risk per unit carry (implying an expensive index protection and poorer compensation for taking on equity tranche risk) as illustrated in **FIGURE 3.11**. This should not be surprising because the delta found by perturbing the spreads by 1 bp is not addressing hedge error minimization or elimination. Therefore, the residual VOD risk (which is not zero even in theory), can be altered by changing the hedging strategy. Such an alteration of hedging will end up producing credit-delta exposure.

Credit Spread

A simple risk assessment paradigm is afforded by knowing the *delta sensitivity* of each instrument to the change in spread of an issuer. Operationally, this is embedded in many risk management systems as a CS01 (that is, the change in *mtm* due to an issuer spread widening by 1 bp). Even for a single CDS, this is a simplification because the duration over which premiums are *expected* to be paid, depends on the issuer risk-neutral default probability, and then nonlinearly on the issuer spreads. As a consequence, the spread widening under more than 1 bp spread move doesn't have to be the product of CS01 and the spread move (in bps). Indeed, if an issuer on which a trading book has sold default protection were to suddenly approach default (unbounded spread rise), the loss is bounded above by the notional amount (minus recovery and adjusting for *mtm*). Such garden-variety nonlinearity is endemic to credit instruments and renders the results of sensitivity-based risk management systems as approximations of the true risks. However, for vanilla credit such approximations are not pernicious. A book that is a net CDS protection purchaser will have its losses under spread tightening understated in a CS01-based system. A book that is a net CDS protection seller will have its losses under extreme moves somewhat exaggerated in a CS01-based system. In either situation, the sign of the *mtm* move incurred due to rapid spread widening or tightening is captured by the CS01 of a vanilla credit book.

For CDO risk management, a CS01-based risk management system is particularly inadequate because of the potential of creating positive-carry trades with little CS01 and with significant negative VOD sensitivity. A trading book with long and short positions on CDOs and CDS (for example, the three model trades analyzed here) can become a seller of default protection on the issuers in the CDO reference pools (that is, exhibit negative VOD to reference names), yet not exhibit any negative CS01 to those issuers, and under extreme spread widening for any of those issuers incurring a significant loss. If all risk management is doing is staring at credit delta or CS01 (or equivalent bond market value exposure), then CDO trading can simply become a pretext to sell default protection without any limit, or recognition of risk-return.

In the model CDO trades examined here, at inception, there is little to no "CS01 risk," yet if spreads were to blow out on any issuer name, the trade incurs a loss. The *mtm* impact of multiple-names spread widening is certainly not the same as the sum of *mtm* impacts of single-name widening. In fact, the simultaneous widening of spreads on many names could result in an *mtm* gain for the strategies shown here (**FIGURES 3.12** and **3.13**). This is referred to as having "positive index gamma." The positive

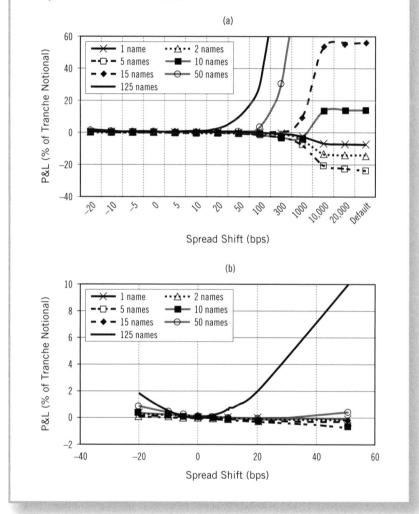

FIGURE **3.12** *Spread Sensitivity of Delta-Hedged Equity Tranche (0% to 3%)*

The issuers are arranged in a decreasing spread order and the top 1,2, ... N names are applied a parallel spread shock (amount depicted on horizontal axis).

Source: CDX.NA.IG.4, March 31, 2005.

index gamma can be of a local nature (for example, if all names widen by 10 bps, the *mtm* impact is positive) and the event of the spreads of all names increasing unboundedly could still be a loss event (**FIGURE 3.14**).

A finer point regarding CS01 hedging of a tranche is whether one em-

Source: CDX.NA.IG.4, March 31, 2005.

FIGURE **3.13** *Spread Sensitivity of Straddle (0% to 3% and 7% to 10%)*

The issuers are arranged in a decreasing spread order and the top 1,2, ... *N* names are applied a parallel spread shock (amount depicted on horizontal axis).

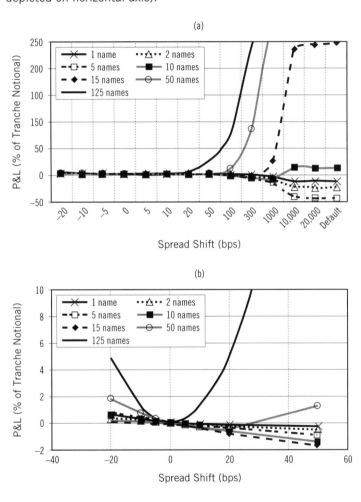

ploys the credit index to hedge or single names. As the index is equally weighted, and the hedge ratios per name (found by bumping individual spreads one at a time) are not identical, employing the index as a CS01 hedge results in slight residual negative and positive CS01 exposures to

FIGURE **3.14** *Spread Sensitivity of Delta-Hedged Senior Mezzanine Tranche (7% to 10%)*

The issuers are arranged in a decreasing spread order and the top 1,2, ... N names are applied a parallel spread shock (amount depicted on horizontal axis).

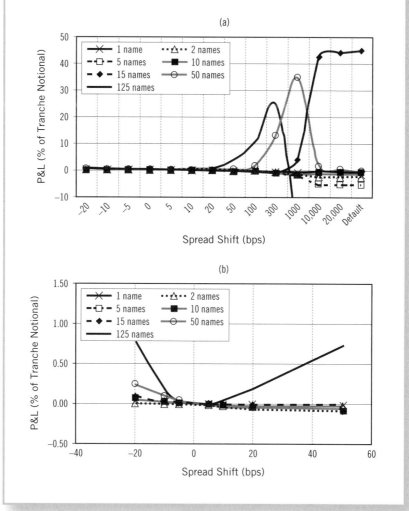

Source: CDX.NA.IG.4, March 31, 2005.

individual names. Whether one bumps all the names 1 bp simultaneously and finds the overall index hedge ratio (in terms of notional), or one bumps individual names to assess individual-hedge ratios and hedges using the index with a notional that equals the sum of the individual-hedge notionals, one arrives at the same point (because convexity does not manifest strongly at 1 bp).

Hedging using the index is popular because of ease efficiency of execution. Periodic single-name hedging can be undertaken as an overlay on top of the index hedging if one desires to maintain a small CS01 exposure per name.

The spread sensitivity computations show that the popular CDO strategies are susceptible to idiosyncratic spread move risks, and any effort to "bucket" spread moves by ratings or sectors and potentially perturb many issuers simultaneously in the same direction is a poor way to assess CDO trading "market risks." The market risk of a CDO strategy can be controlled by the propensity of spreads to not move together and, therefore, the broad brush coherent moves based on either sector or ratings is misleading. While there can be index or sector factor drivers for spread moves, a name-specific spread time series (modeled or historically sampled) is a prerequisite for articulating a hedging strategy and for assessing a synthetic CDO trading value at risk (VaR). While a CS01-based VaR can be uninformative for synthetic CDOs (by not addressing convexity and correlation risk), a VaR based on broad index moves can be even more misleading because the positive-carry strategies encounter losses under spread twists and not necessarily under coherent parallel shocks that are more amenable to traditional "market-risk" scenarios.

Tranche Pricing Correlation

For illustration purposes, all the sensitivities shown previously did not involve any changes to the implied correlation of the tranches. The tranche implied correlation provides the market participants a way to express their views on model assumptions, which are: (1) static spread term structure, (2) normal copula, (3) fixed recovery, and (4) deterministic asset-correlation structure. Indeed, there is no way to separate the effect of all these assumptions once they have been thrown into the kitchen sink of implied correlation. To be sure, correlation is not the only uncertain variable in portfolio credit derivative pricing. Recovery uncertainty and recovery-default correlation are long outstanding features that do not find systematic treatment even in single-name CDS pricing practice.

The need for different implied correlation values to be input to price different tranches across the capital structure is referred to as the correlation skew. The correlation skew can be at least qualitatively explained with even a small set of the kitchen sink ingredients. For example, the correlation delta and convexity (**FIGURE 3.15**) on their own qualitatively support the existence of the skew, and it would be quite hard to argue that asset correlation inputs into pricing models are perfectly knowable.

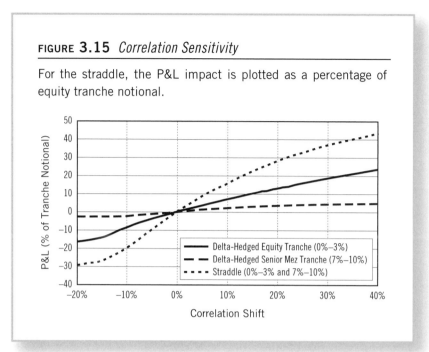

FIGURE **3.15** *Correlation Sensitivity*

For the straddle, the P&L impact is plotted as a percentage of equity tranche notional.

Legend:
— Delta-Hedged Equity Tranche (0%–3%)
– – Delta-Hedged Senior Mez Tranche (7%–10%)
∙∙∙∙ Straddle (0%–3% and 7%–10%)

Y-axis: P&L (% of Tranche Notional)
X-axis: Correlation Shift

Based on uncertainty of asset correlation input for a correlation model, a tranche with a default payment leg with positive correlation convexity and an increasing function of correlation can be expected to price at a correlation above the historical average (based on Jensen's inequality). The super senior tranche can have this behavior. A tranche with a default payment leg with positive correlation convexity and that is a decreasing function of correlation can be expected to price at a correlation below the historical average. An equity tranche can have this behavior. If the tranche contingent leg was nonmonotonic in correlation, it could price at more than one implied correlation.

A tranche with a default payment leg with negative correlation convexity and that is an increasing function of correlation can be expected to price at a correlation below the average correlation, based on uncertain asset correlations. A tranche with a default payment leg with negative correlation convexity and that is a decreasing function of correlation can be expected to price at a correlation above the historical average correlation. These rudimentary correlation convexity arguments are sufficient to explain the compound correlation skew qualitatively. Asset and default correlation are not deterministically knowable parameters. Under significant correlation convexity, it is inconceivable for the market to price different tranches of the same structure at the same correlation.

As the correlation is a pricing variable, CDO trades are exposed to the market risk of that pricing parameter changing. Interestingly, just as the default risk was shown to be an increasing function of the initial trade carry of the three CDO trades analyzed here, the correlation sensitivity (Figure 3.15) is also an increasing function of the initial trade carry. The highest carry trade, the straddle, has the highest correlation sensitivity (moving both the equity and mezzanine/senior tranche correlation simultaneously). The equity tranche trade has the second highest correlation sensitivity and the second highest carry. The mezzanine/senior tranche trade has the lowest carry and the lowest correlation sensitivity.

Trading P&L Case Study

Sell Equity Tranche Protection Position on CDX.NA.IG

While the previous analysis dissected the residual risks in CS01- or delta-hedged trades, and presents interesting risk-return trade-offs (carry versus VOD, spread, and implied correlation sensitivity), it does not show how different components of the P&L evolve over time in response to simultaneous changes in market variables (that is, issuer spreads and implied correlations). To examine in greater depth how a combination of market variable changes influences the risk-return of synthetic CDO trades, we examine the components of the trading P&L: (1) cash component; (2) mark-to-market component. The change in a trading book's wealth is given by the sum of these components:

$$\Delta W(t) = C(t) + mtm(t)$$

Under the assumption that the cash flows received/incurred accrue at the short risk-free rate, we have

$$C(t) = \sum_{i:t_i \le t} c_i \exp\left[\int_{t_i}^{t} r(\tau) d\tau\right]$$

The cash flows incurred at times t_i are denoted by ci, and $r(\tau)$, which is the risk-free, short-term interest rate. The mark-to-market component responds to evolving spreads, pricing model correlations, and defaults.

A trade on the CDX.NA.IG pool is initiated on March 22, 2005. Using historical time series for on-the-run quotes on CDX.NA.IG, index spread, and single-name spreads, we display the P&L of different types of trades (unhedged and delta hedged) and the impact of rebalancing on

TABLE 3.2 *Spread Measures*

Cross-sectional average spread for a CDO reference pool with N_n names for term T

DEFINITION
$$\tilde{s}\left(t_k, T\right) \equiv \frac{1}{N_n} \sum_{i=1}^{N_n} s_i\left(t_k, T\right)$$

Cross-sectional spread dispersion

DEFINITION
$$\tilde{\sigma}_s\left(t_k, T\right) \equiv \sqrt{\frac{1}{N_n} \sum_{i=1}^{N_n} \left(s_i\left(t_k, T\right) - \tilde{s}\left(t_k, T\right)\right)^2}$$

Normalized cross-sectional spread dispersion

DEFINITION
$$\tilde{\sigma}_s\left(t_k, T\right) \big/ \tilde{s}\left(t_k, T\right)$$

Spread change over n days

DEFINITION
$$\Delta s_i(t_k, T; n) \equiv s_i\left(t_{k+n}, T\right) - s_i\left(t_k, T\right)$$

Average of spread change over n days with N_d day dataset

DEFINITION
$$\overline{\Delta s_i}(T; n) = \frac{1}{\left(N_d - n\right)} \sum_{j=1}^{N_d - n} \Delta s_i(t_j, T, n)$$

Standard deviation of spread change over n days with N_d day data

DEFINITION
$$\sigma_{\Delta s_i}(T; n) = \sqrt{\frac{1}{\left(N_d - n\right)} \sum_{j=1}^{N_d - n} \left(\Delta s_i(t_j, T, n) - \overline{\Delta s_i}(T; n)\right)^2}$$

Pair-wise realized correlation of spread change over n days

DEFINITION
$$\rho_{ij}(T; n) \equiv$$
$$\frac{\sum_{m=1}^{N_d - n} \left(\Delta s_i\left(t_m, T; n\right) - \overline{\Delta s_i}(T; n)\right)\left(\Delta s_j\left(t_m, T; n\right) - \overline{\Delta s_j}(T; n)\right)}{\sigma_{\Delta s_i} \sigma_{\Delta s_j} \times \left(N_d - n\right)}$$

Cross-sectional average realized correlation of spread change over n days

DEFINITION
$$\tilde{\rho}(T; n) = \frac{2}{N_n\left(N_n - 1\right)} \sum_{i=2}^{N_n} \sum_{j=1}^{i-1} \rho_{ij}(T, n)$$

P&L volatility. To interpret these results, we examine many different measures of credit spread (**TABLE 3.2**) in addition to the implied correlation time series for the equity tranche.

Time Decay-Carry View at Execution

If there are no market moves, as time passes by and the trade matures, what would be the wealth of the trader at different points in time? The cash component of trader's wealth is made up of the initial payment received to sell protection and ongoing premium payments. If a hedge is in place, then there are ongoing payments for the hedge. The up-front payment on the CDO tranche and the received running premium payments (netted with premium payments to purchase hedge) are assumed to accrete and grow at short-term, risk-free rates. The initial *mtm* on the CDO equity tranche is negative due to the up-front payment, but it decays with time due to the decreased expected contingent payments over smaller maturities. **FIGURE 3.16a** depicts the time-decay view of P&L on a sell equity tranche protection position.

FIGURE 3.16b depicts the time-decay view of P&L on a buy CDS index protection (that is, the CDS index position needed to delta hedge CDO equity tranche sell protection position at inception depicted in Figure 3.16a). The *mtm* component of the CDS index hedge is zero at inception (fairly priced with no up-front payment) and at maturity. The *mtm* of the CDS index hedge may not be zero in between inception and maturity, depending on the credit spread term-structure and the manner in which time decay is assessed. For the combined CDO tranche with CDS index hedge position, the P&L components are shown in **FIGURE 3.16c**. These time-decay views of P&L are assessed by decreasing the maturity of the transaction (from five years at inception). Another view of time decay is by rolling the transaction on the forward curves (interest rates and credit spread).

Both the unhedged sell equity protection trade (Figure 3.16a) and the CS01-hedged trade (Figure 3.16c) are *positive carry* insofar as in the absence of market moves the protection seller's wealth increases with time. Both the unhedged sell equity protection trade and the CS01-hedged trade have negative marginal VOD sensitivities (Figure 3.5), with the unhedged trade having larger carry and a more negative VOD sensitivity than the CS01-hedged trade. Therefore, both the unhedged sell equity protection trade and the CS01-hedged trade represent long credit positions.

P&L Components with Market Moves

In the long-only (sell equity tranche protection) trade or the statically delta-hedged trade, the cash component is not influenced by movements in credit spreads (**FIGURE 3.17a**).

FIGURE 3.16 *Time-Decay View on Trade Date for Sell Equity Tranche Protection Position*

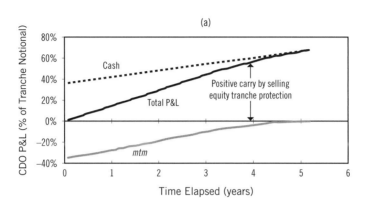

(a)

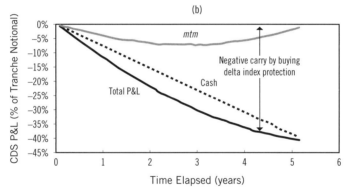

(b)

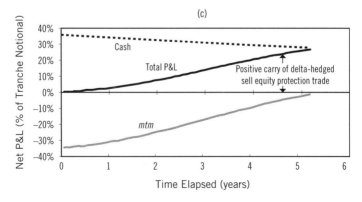

(c)

A sell equity protection position results in receiving an up-front payment and ongoing running premium payments (which have been accrued continuously here). Delta hedging of the equity tranche results in the running net premium to be negative (cash outflow), on top of the positive up-front payment. Dynamic delta hedging can result in accretion of extra cash or a depletion of cash relative to the statically hedged case depending on whether positive spread index gamma dominates or whether negative idiosyncratic spread gamma dominates (that is, in scenarios where the pool spreads move coherently between hedging intervals, additional cash is accreted, relative to scenarios where the spreads disperse [low realized correlation] over the hedging interval).

The *mtm* of the trade is influenced by movements in credit spreads and implied correlation, on top of time decay (**FIGURE 3.17b**). The total P&L (cash plus *mtm*) is displayed in **FIGURE 3.17c**.

The unhedged sell equity tranche protection position is an outright long credit-delta exposure and is also long correlation; therefore, it suffers a deep blow when spreads widen on the average and the equity tranche implied correlation falls. A short credit-hedging position dampens the *mtm* fluctuations (and reduces the cash component of the P&L). It turns out that a static hedge (CS01 hedge using the index at inception) ends up performing not too different from daily CS01-hedged trade (employing the index to hedge). The less frequently hedged trade (delta hedge every two weeks and two months) happens to perform better than the daily or statically hedged trade (Figure 3.17c). We provide an interpretation of the P&L moves based on market variables next.

Role of Index Spread, Spread Dispersion, and Implied Correlation

A sharp P&L drawdown event for the sell equity tranche trade (initiated in March 2005 on CDX.NA.IG) occurred in May 2005. This was associated with a widening of the index average spread, a widening of the index cross-sectional dispersion of spreads, and a sudden drop in the implied correlation for the equity tranche (**FIGURE 3.18**). Both index spread widening and increase in dispersion had built up over April, and then in May there was a sharp drop in implied correlation.

Even the delta-hedged equity tranche trade experienced a significant P&L drawdown despite being CS01 hedged using the index. This is because of the increase in cross-sectional spread dispersion in the index and the concomitant decrease in the equity tranche implied correlation. Index average spread widening, increase of cross-sectional dispersion, and drop of implied correlation tend to happen together (see **TABLE 3.3** and **FIGURES 3.19** and **3.20**). The scatter plot of the equity implied correlation versus spread dispersion (Figure 3.20) suggests that the market developed

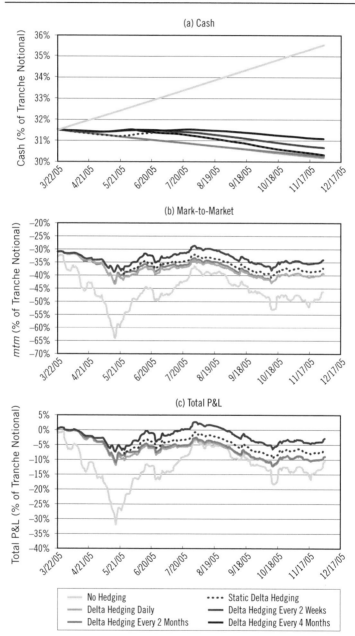

FIGURE 3.17 *Components of P&L for Sample CDX.NA.IG.4 Sell Equity Protection Trade*

(a) Cash

(b) Mark-to-Market

(c) Total P&L

No Hedging
Delta Hedging Daily
Delta Hedging Every 2 Months
Static Delta Hedging
Delta Hedging Every 2 Weeks
Delta Hedging Every 4 Months

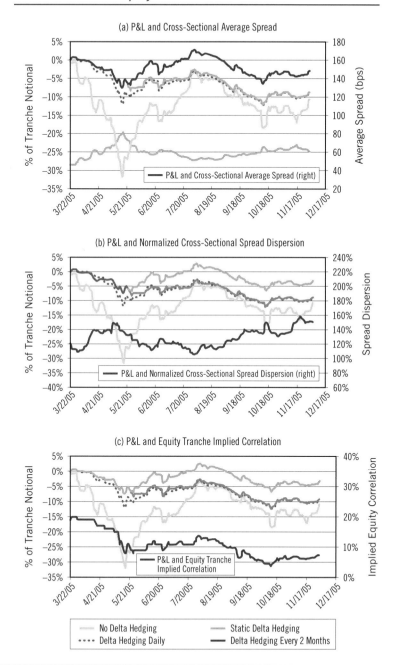

FIGURE **3.18** *P&L and Risk Factors for Sample CDX.NA.IG.4 Sell Equity Protection Trade*

(a) P&L and Cross-Sectional Average Spread

P&L and Cross-Sectional Average Spread (right)

(b) P&L and Normalized Cross-Sectional Spread Dispersion

P&L and Normalized Cross-Sectional Spread Dispersion (right)

(c) P&L and Equity Tranche Implied Correlation

P&L and Equity Tranche Implied Correlation

No Delta Hedging   Static Delta Hedging
Delta Hedging Daily   Delta Hedging Every 2 Months

TABLE **3.3** *Correlation Between Index Spread Measures and Equity Tranche Implied Correlation*

	CROSS-SECTIONAL AVERAGE SPREAD	NORMALIZED CROSS-SECTION SPREAD DISPERSION	EQUITY IMPLIED CORRELATION
Cross-sectional average speed	1		
Normalized cross-section spread dispersion	65%	1	
Equity implied correlation	−45%	−45%	1

Source: CDX.NA.IG.4

FIGURE **3.19** *Time Series of Cross-Sectional Average Spread, Cross-Sectional Spread Dispersion (Normalized by Average Spread), and Equity Tranche Implied Correlation*

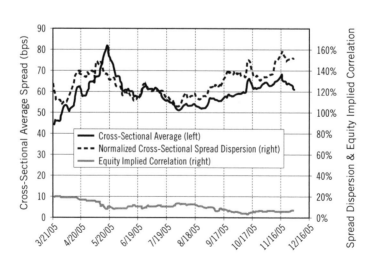

Source: CDX.NA.IG.4

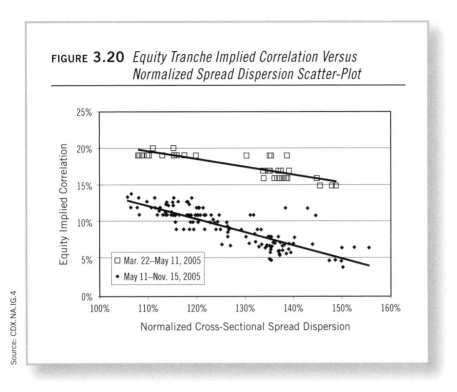

FIGURE **3.20** *Equity Tranche Implied Correlation Versus Normalized Spread Dispersion Scatter-Plot*

a new realization of the vulnerability of the sell equity protection trade to pool idiosyncrasies in May.

The response of the implied correlation pricing parameter to market spread moves can be interpreted as follows. As the index spread widens, those market players who have a leveraged long exposure to the index via an unhedged equity tranche protection sell position, and those who have a heightened exposure to idiosyncratic spread moves via CS01-hedged sell equity tranche protection positions, incur losses. In response to these losses, they either try to close out their position (by taking an opposing position) or demand greater compensation for taking on the risk. The increased demand for buying equity tranche protection and higher asking price for selling equity tranche protection both manifest as a downward move in the equity tranche implied correlation parameter.

This empirical feature of spread dispersion being associated with index widening and equity implied correlation decreasing underlines the inadequacy of employing CS01 as the primary risk-monitoring tool for synthetic CDO trades. A delta-hedged trade will not exhibit any CS01 and not prepare anyone for losses that will occur when the index spread widens (despite little CS01 exposure): these losses are inflicted by idiosyncratic spread movements and the associated decrease in equity implied correlation. If a CDO tranche is thought to simply be a collection of single-name credit instruments (albeit with the correct individual CS01), one is simply not prepared for the downside risks associated with idiosyncratic spread flare outs and implied correlation movements.

Tales of poor P&L attribution from credit delta risk factors and surprise and fear associated with P&L marking and risk assessment abound in the broker-dealer and hedge fund community transacting in synthetic CDOs. The experiences in 2005 have crystallized the fallacy of measuring synthetic CDO risk by systems that were built primarily for single-name instruments and have also highlighted the importance of assessing P&L risk scenarios under a comprehensive set of spread moves, with single-name granularity, and correlation move scenarios, in addition to the MC default risk described in previous sections.

Realized Correlation of Spread Moves and Delta Hedging

A measure of the tendency of spreads to move together (or not) is expressed by the "realized correlation," which for a pair of names is the correlation of the changes in spreads over different intervals. This measure is defined in Table 3.2. To calculate the correlation between the changes of spreads for a pair of obligors from a time series requires a time window, which is taken to be the CDX.NA.IG.4 life (from March 22 onwards). This creates a pair-wise realized correlation matrix of spread change over different time intervals, and the average of those correlations (off-diagonal elements) is shown in **FIGURE 3.21**. The spreads show a tendency to have more coherent moves over longer time intervals (for example, two months) compared to shorter time intervals (daily). For example, the daily spread changes have an average correlation of about 16%, whereas the correlation of spread changes over two weeks rises to 35%, and over two months it becomes about 40%. Beyond intervals of two months, the realized correlation appears to fall (although that inference is relatively less reliable considering the time averaging window to infer correlations is approximately nine months long).

The relationship of realized correlation with time interval helps interpret the performance of the hedging strategy, where hedging every two weeks ends up with a more favorable P&L outcome relative to daily delta hedging, and hedging every two months ends up even better (Figure 3.17). This is a demonstration of how delta hedging a sell equity tranche position can result in a monetization of positive index spread gamma, when spreads move coherently over the hedging interval. In the extremely artificial case where there is a perfect coherence of spread moves (and the implied cor-

Source: CDX.NA.IG.4, March 22, 2005 through November 15, 2005.

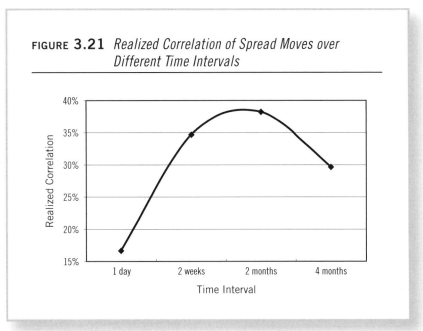

FIGURE **3.21** *Realized Correlation of Spread Moves over Different Time Intervals*

relation does not move), the mere act of delta hedging would result in perpetual P&L gains. In the more realistic case, idiosyncratic spread moves and associated movements in the implied correlation parameters compete with coherent spread moves, and more frequent delta hedging does not guarantee the least volatile P&L profile and definitely not the most favorable P&L outcome.

There are two important features of the static spread-based copula models (currently widely being used to mark-to-market CDO tranches) that need to be kept in mind when interpreting hedge performance results: (1) spread dynamics are not a part of that standard pricing model and (2) the conception of that model has not been accompanied by any demonstration of option replication and hedge error elimination (even in theory). It is not surprising that the implied correlation pricing parameter associated with that model has embedded in it a risk premium for idiosyncratic spread moves. A more desirable state of affairs for the pricing model would be one which explicitly describes objective measure of the CDO reference pool at the constituent level (spread dispersion, jumps, jump to default, recovery uncertainty, correlation) and constructs a hedging strategy to achieve an objective, with uncertainty elimination being the cornerstone for expounding the arbitrage-free price.

Even though less frequent delta hedging can result in a monetization of high realized correlation of spread changes, if that transpires, less frequent delta hedging also exposes one to jump to default (or single-name spread blowout) risk to a greater degree than if one were delta hedging more frequently. Over larger time intervals, there is a greater chance of a single name undergoing dramatic credit deterioration than over a shorter interval. Therefore, to examine the trade-offs between hedging frequency and total risks (spread, correlation, defaults), one needs to integrate a name-specific spread model with a default model. In this work, we have simply examined the historical realization of spreads, and the previous section on default risk entertained an MC simulation of defaults separately.

Summary

Credit Event Risk Versus Credit "Delta" Risk

It was shown here that positive-carry synthetic CDO trades (that is, the trader's wealth increases with time in the absence of any market moves) can be created with little CS01 risk while being long credit exposures (having a VOD that is negative for all names in the CDO reference pool). Additionally, for these positive-carry CS01 neutral trades, the loss due to default sensitivity (VOD) tends to be an increasing function of the initial carry on the trade. This is different from a traditional portfolio credit where the sign of the credit delta exposure (CS01) and default exposure (VOD) tends to be the same.

Systematic Versus Idiosyncratic Risks

Single-name spread convexity, while providing an important measure of risk, is not sufficient to understand CDO risk return. This is because if the spreads of all names widen, the result is a P&L gain for the positive carry strategies described here, despite them incurring losses if any single name were to become credit impaired. Therefore, the "index spread convexity" can have a different sign from the "idiosyncratic spread convexity." This idiosyncratic spread convexity can cause losses for the popular positive-carry trade when spreads do not move in tandem. The implied correlation for the equity tranche has an inverse dependence on spread dispersion, and that further exacerbates the losses experienced by positive-carry trades when spreads disperse, as experienced in 2005.

Similarly, the impact of multiple defaults is different from the sum of the impacts of single-name defaults. In fact, for the delta-hedged CDO trades, multiple defaults can result in P&L gains despite the marginal impact of each individual default being a significant loss.

Tranche Pricing Correlation Risks

Positive-carry CDO trades are, in general, long correlation. That implied correlation of the CDO tranche can undergo sudden changes, as witnessed in May and September in 2005. These changes have been associated with sector credit quality moves (for example, autos in May) and specific trade flows (leveraged super senior trades in September). These fluctuations in implied correlation reflect an evolving market as it grapples with the risk of tranched credit risk in long-short portfolios. These fluctuations in implied correlation also reflect how the market becomes more or less risk averse depending on how coherently the spreads move. There is a discernable correlation between the equity tranche implied correlation and the cross-sectional spread dispersion measure. This is perhaps due to the market participants that are long correlation (for example, sellers of equity tranche protection) incurring losses when spread dispersion is high. These market participants, on incurring losses when spreads disperse, become more risk averse and, therefore, start asking for a greater compensation for selling first loss protection.

As the hedging and risk management strategy evolves, the correlation markets will "learn" to coexist with the volatility markets (for example, swaptions) and the differences in index and single-name implied volatilities should provide some constraint on the implied correlation markets. As these two markets start to transmit to each other, the pricing modeling paradigm will be pushed towards directly addressing replication and hedging errors (accounting for coherent and idiosyncratic spread moves and credit events) as a precursor to pricing rather than as an afterthought.

Risk-Aggregation and Reporting Regimes

Marginal and linear sensitivity-based risk aggregation is reasonable insofar as every trade's marginal contribution to the overall risks and risk capital can be assessed. However, while a risk management framework based on linear sensitivities such as *credit delta* may be adequate for relatively linear credit instruments (bonds, CDS, portfolios of bonds and CDS), it is not adequate for strongly nonlinear instruments such as CDOs. Many popular synthetic CDO trades do not even show up on the radar of such traditional risk management schemes. Risk management will have to evolve significantly to deal with the risks associated with synthetic CDOs that can manifest due to spread gamma (index spread gamma and idiosyncratic spread gamma often having opposite signs) and implied correlation fluctuations. Risk reports will have to stop equating credit delta risk exposures with credit event risk exposures because CDO trades may not exhibit any credit delta risk at inception, and yet may be long all the credits underlying the CDO pool from a credit event perspective (that is, negative VOD).

The risk-systems challenge is to replace highly convenient marginal and linear sensitivity-based approaches with a trade-strategy cognizant approach that requires: (1) resolving single-name credit description without any bucketing (or artificial separation of "index" and "specific" risks) and (2) a revaluation of the CDO positions under historical and/or simulated scenarios (including defaults) and time series.

CHAPTER 4

Integrating Credit Hedge Funds into a Portfolio of Investments

RICHARD HORWITZ AND ERIN ROYE SIMPSON

The objective of this chapter is to address the behavior of credit hedge funds from the perspective of an institutional investor. Investment organizations, in particular hedge funds, are generally structured as "silos" of specialization: narrow in focus but extremely deep in their expertise of the specific strategy that is being executed. The challenge for investors is to invest in multiple and diverse silos and to construct a "risk-efficient" portfolio of both traditional and alternative investments. Therefore, this chapter will address how credit funds can be incorporated into a broadly diversified portfolio.

This chapter will explore eight key topics related to credit hedge funds from the investor's perspective:

1. Credit hedge fund strategies
2. Performance profiles
3. Risk management and transparency
4. Correlations and diversification
5. Portfolio construction
6. Liquidity and leverage
7. Valuation
8. Sustainability and scalability

Each topic will be discussed in a separate section of the chapter.

The views expressed herein reflect those of the authors and are not necessarily those of Merrill Lynch & Co. Inc. or its affiliates.

Credit Hedge Fund Strategies

We estimate that between six hundred and eight hundred of the total universe of eight thousand hedge funds are "credit" funds. **FIGURE 4.1** displays the distribution of credit hedge funds by strategy. The majority of the statistics cited in this chapter are based on data from January 1990 through December 2006 provided by Hedge Fund Research (HFR). (All statistics are calculated since inception, or January 1990 if the fund predates that cutoff.) However, neither HFR, nor other hedge fund databases, separately identify the newer, niche credit strategies of direct lending and structured credit. The authors accumulated data on these strategies. The following is a description of the major credit hedge fund strategies:

❑ ***Emerging market debt.*** Emerging market funds take long biased positions in emerging market debt. These funds take long exposures to both the interest rates and credit spreads of these markets. Emerging market funds sometimes hedge interest rates with G-7 sovereign debt (especially Treasuries) or high-quality emerging market debt, such as Brady bonds. HFR includes 125 of these funds.

❑ ***Convertible arbitrage.*** Convertible arbitrage funds take long biased positions in corporate convertible bonds or distressed convertible debt ("busted converts"), and selectively hedge these exposures with interest rate instruments, credit derivatives, and equities. The convertible bonds have interest rate, credit, equity, and equity volatility exposures

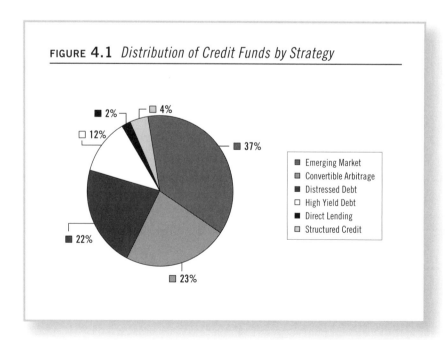

FIGURE 4.1 *Distribution of Credit Funds by Strategy*

- 4%
- ■ 2%
- ☐ 12%
- ■ 37%
- ■ 22%
- ■ 23%

- ■ Emerging Market
- ☐ Convertible Arbitrage
- ■ Distressed Debt
- ☐ High Yield Debt
- ■ Direct Lending
- ☐ Structured Credit

(nondollar bonds also have currency exposures), and any or all of these exposures can be hedged. These funds can also short the convertible bond ("Chinese") and hedge their short positions as described previously. In general, convertible arbitrage represents more of a volatility play than a credit play. HFR includes seventy-five of these funds.

❑ ***Distressed debt.*** Distressed debt funds take long biased positions in distressed debt or bank loans. They often try to hedge their exposures by shorting higher quality, more liquid debt securities, particularly high-yield bonds. These funds can participate in varying phases of the bankruptcy cycle on either a passive or active basis. HFR includes seventy-two of these funds.

❑ ***High-yield debt.*** High-yield funds take long and short positions that seek to capture the issue-specific misevaluations within the high-yield debt market. The issue selection in these funds is generally driven by in-depth fundamental research. Some of these funds employ the Merton model and are seeking to arbitrage the inefficiencies between the debt and equity markets. HFR includes forty of these funds.

❑ ***Direct lending.*** Direct lending funds directly originate nonsecuritized loans, which are often collateralized by receivables or inventories. These loans are long only and have a short duration (almost always less than two years and generally less than a year). The loans are generally issued to subprime borrowers, who operate in specialized niches that have been ignored by traditional financing companies. Such a fund is equivalent to being a bank. These funds are not separately identified by HFR, but we estimate there are between ten and twenty of them.

❑ ***Structured credit.*** Structured credit funds take long biased positions in structured debt, including asset-backed securities (ABSs) and collateralized debt obligations (CDOs). These funds generally invest in lower quality, more complex, and less liquid tranches. However, some structured credit funds invest in higher quality pools, enhancing their relatively low returns with leverage. These funds are not separately identified by HFR, but we estimate there are between twenty and thirty of them in existence.

Performance Profiles

With the exception of convertible arbitrage (discussed later), credit hedge funds have generated attractive returns over the last several years, although they have consistently declined (**FIGURE 4.2**).

Furthermore, as **FIGURE 4.3** demonstrates, the risk-adjusted returns (average Sharpe ratio) have been very appealing as well. The newer strategies (shorter average track record length) of direct lending and structured

FIGURE **4.2** *Credit Hedge Fund Returns by Style*

	2003	2004	2005	2006	2003–2006
Emerging market	39.4%	18.4%	20.9%	24.3%	25.5%
Convertible arbitrage	9.9%	1.2%	–1.9%	12.2%	5.2%
Distressed debt	29.6%	18.9%	8.4%	15.8%	17.9%
High yield	21.3%	10.5%	5.1%	10.7%	11.8%
Direct lending	12.9%	10.2%	10.4%	10.8%	11.0%
Structured credit	26.5%	19.6%	10.8%	10.6%	16.7%

FIGURE **4.3** *Average Performance of Credit Hedge Funds by Style*

	RECORD LENGTH (MONTHS)	RETURN	STANDARD DEVIATION	SHARPE RATIO
Emerging market	78	24.7%	29.1%	.98
Convertible arbitrage	70	12.9%	9.6%	1.01
Distressed debt	68	23.7%	14.6%	1.94
High yield	61	25.9%	19.8%	1.80
Direct lending	49	12.7%	.9%	15.91
Structured credit	35	20.6%	6.5%	4.48

credit enjoy the best average risk-adjusted returns, measured by the Sharpe ratio since inception. These both represent niche strategies that are not separately identified by HFR. Because the credit strategies are relatively illiquid, the volatility (standard deviation) of their returns is understated (discussed later) and consequently, their risk-adjusted returns are overstated.

Risk Management and Transparency

In *Hedge Fund Risk Fundamentals: Solving the Risk Management and Transparency Challenge* by Richard Horwitz (Bloomberg Press, 2004) the introduction stated: "The fund manager looks at a single fund through a microscope, and the investor searches the universe of funds through a telescope." Let's explore this metaphor a little closer. Through a microscope a physicist can see individual molecules moving in Brownian motion. When these molecules combine to create a planet, an astronomer can view this planet revolving around its star through a telescope. However, the telescope will not permit the astronomer to view the movement of the molecules that make up this planet. The physicist and astronomer require very different pieces of equipment to achieve very different objectives.

Similarly, credit specialists within a hedge fund require a very different set of tools and analytics than an investor who seeks a fundamental understanding of the overall risk of the credit hedge fund, and how to integrate it into a diversified portfolio of investments. Since being long credit is effectively being short an option, credit specialists view credit as "event risk." Therefore, they focus on measuring the risk of specific events (for example, downgrades, defaults, restructurings) related to individual issues. Credit analytic systems such as KMV and CreditGrades all employ this concept of event risk. In contrast, investors in a portfolio of funds diversify away the risk of individual events across diverse holdings. For example, if an investor invested in a diversified portfolio of hedge funds (let's say twenty funds) and two or even three funds had holdings in a company such as WorldCom or Enron, which rapidly fell into bankruptcy, the potential loss exposure would only be 20 to 60 basis points (10% to 20% of the portfolio losing potentially 2% to 3% per portfolio). Investors should be significantly more worried about the synchronous behavior of events within a fund or style (for example, decline in the equity market or the systematic tightening of credit spreads), and even more importantly, across styles and investments (for example, the fall of 1998).

Therefore, the primary objective of investors is to manage the synchronous or structural behavior of their investments. Risk factor frameworks provide such a fundamental understanding of structural risks. That is why they are employed by an estimated 75% of traditional (long-only) equity managers. Furthermore, that is why they are broadly used by investors in "style analysis" (for example, Morningstar) to compare and analyze traditional mutual funds. However, traditional risk factor frameworks have been broadly limited to long-only portfolios, primarily of equities. While established solutions (Barra, Northfield) have provided a rich and insightful solution to managing traditional equity portfolios, they have not adequately supported the management of diverse portfolios. They have generally not been used by traditional credit managers and have made virtually no inroads into credit hedge funds.

Even VaR, the sell-side risk management solution that has made inroads into some hedge funds, has also not found acceptance in credit hedge funds (VaR has primarily been used by global macro hedge funds, which are similar to the prop desks for which the technique was developed). VaR works in highly liquid strategies with very good price discovery: credit hedge fund strategies generally satisfy neither of these conditions. In strategies where VaR systems have worked, they are useful in measuring the risk. However, they do not explain the source of risk and, therefore, cannot provide the critical understanding of structural behavior, called risk transparency, that investors require.

The challenge has been to develop a comprehensive credit risk model that explains structural behavior of credit funds. Risk Fundamentals® (a risk management, transparency, portfolio construction, and performance attribution system)[1] has achieved this as a component of a comprehensive risk factor framework, designed to support both traditional and alternative investments. The framework integrates equity, interest rate, credit, physical commodity, currency, and real estate risks. We present the credit risk factor framework used by Risk Fundamentals as an example of how risk factors can be used in credit hedge funds to understand structural risk. A separate set of credit risk factors are provided for each currency. The primary credit risk factors of each set are the market risk factors:

❑ *Spread shift.* The synchronous movement of credit spreads across all maturities and all credit qualities. This is not defined as a parallel shift, as spreads do not tend to move in parallel across maturities or credit qualities but rather in some multiplicative relationship relative to one another. The spread shift has been defined as the 5-year key rate of the benchmark spreads (Industrial BBB for the United States). Sensitivities to this risk factor have been established for each key rate by credit curve.

❑ *Correlation.* The synchronous movement of correlations across securities in basket trades.

Two secondary credit risk factors focus on the term structure of credit:

❑ *Spread twist.* This measures the tendency of the term structure of credit spreads to deviate from the average multiplicative relationship across key rates. The spread twist has been defined as the 1-year benchmark spreads orthogonalized by the spread shift. Sensitivities to this risk factor have been established for each key rate by credit curve.

❑ *Spread butterfly.* This measures the tendency of the term structure of credit spreads to deviate from the relationship defined by the spread shift and spread twist across key rates. The spread butterfly has been defined as the 30-year benchmark spreads orthogonalized by both the spread shift and the spread twist. Sensitivities to this risk factor have been established for each key rate greater than five years by credit curve.

An additional two secondary credit risk factors capture the degree that spreads do not consistently respond proportionately across all credit qualities. Depending on whether the rating of a credit instrument is better or worse than the benchmark, one of the following two credit risk factors is also used:

❑ *High-grade spread.* This measures the tendency of spreads of high-quality credits (bonds with credit quality equal to or better than the benchmark) to deviate from the average multiplicative relationship across credit qualities. The high-grade spread has been defined as the industrial AA 5-year benchmark spreads orthogonalized by the spread shift, spread twist, and the spread butterfly. Sensitivities to this risk factor have been established for all credit spreads of quality equal to or higher than the benchmark curve by key rate.

❑ *Junk spread.* This measures the tendency of spreads of low-quality credits (bonds with credit quality lower than the benchmark) to deviate from the average multiplicative relationship across credit qualities. The junk spread has been defined as the industrial B 5-year benchmark spreads orthogonalized by the spread shift, spread twist, and the spread butterfly. Sensitivities to this risk factor have been established for all credit spreads of quality lower than the benchmark curve by key rate.

Out of these six credit risk factors, a bond has sensitivities to a minimum of three (shift, twist, and either high-grade or junk since the bond will only be sensitive to butterfly if it has a maturity of greater than five years), and a maximum of four (including butterfly). The residual returns are recognized as idiosyncratic risk. Idiosyncratic returns cannot be attributed to a specific type of risk (for example, equity, interest, credit, currency) and the idiosyncratic behavior cannot be exclusively linked to a specific risk factor (for example, a yen-denominated convertible bond has exposure to equity, equity volatility, interest, credit, and currency risk factors).

Having defined the credit risk factor framework, Risk Fundamentals developed a methodology to map specific credit instruments to this credit risk infrastructure. Doing so required the application of space-age technology. We will step back to our prior discussion of telescopes, in this case the Hubble Space Telescope. To develop a well-behaved set of risk factor sensitivities, we have utilized specialized "image analysis" technology explicitly developed for astronomers (fortunately, Erin Simpson was formerly a research analyst at the Space Telescope Science Institute prior to joining the

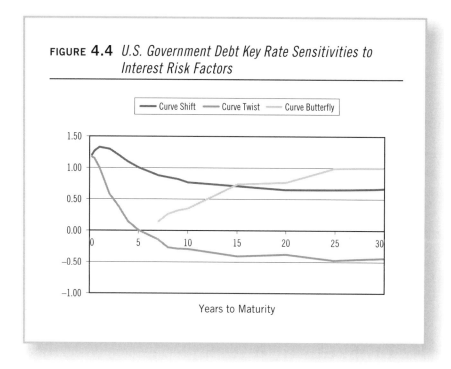

FIGURE **4.4** *U.S. Government Debt Key Rate Sensitivities to Interest Risk Factors*

financial services industry). Our ability to do this is another benefit of the space program, beyond those of CorningWare and Tang.

In developing sensitivities of government bonds to the interest rate risk factors, the high level of price discovery and consistent behavior of Treasuries permitted simple multivariate linear regression to be applied repeatedly to separately map each key rate to the interest-rate risk factors. As shown in **FIGURE 4.4**, the relationships demonstrate high levels of explanatory power (average R^2 of 0.99 for maturities of one year or greater) for each key rate and a well-behaved (monotonic) progression of regression coefficients across the term structure (key rates).

A similar methodology applied to credit spreads resulted in lower levels of explanatory power (average R^2 of 0.64). Furthermore, the progression of coefficients across the term structure was not nearly as well behaved. All five of the risk factors demonstrated considerably irregular "sensitivity surfaces." These surfaces represent the sensitivity of each relevant credit quality and key rate to the particular risk factor in question. **FIGURE 4.5** demonstrates this irregular data, using shift and high-grade as examples. The x-axis of these plots represents credit quality, which is quantified as the average credit spread over the history of the regression for each credit series. The y-axis represents the key rate, and the z-axis shows the sensitivity to the particular risk factor for each credit quality-key rate relationship.

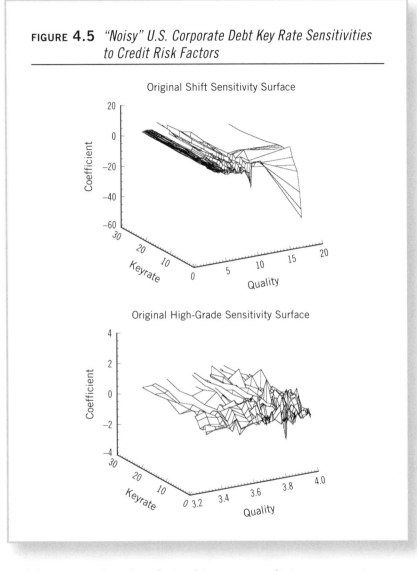

FIGURE **4.5** *"Noisy" U.S. Corporate Debt Key Rate Sensitivities to Credit Risk Factors*

The reasons that the relationship across credit instruments is not as well behaved include:

❏ Price discovery of corporate bonds is significantly worse than that of government bonds.

❏ Issue-specific idiosyncratic behavior pollutes fundamental relationships.

❏ Corporate bond data often require material "adjustments" (particularly for embedded options) that can result in anomalies.

❏ Credit curves are synthesized from disparate issuers.

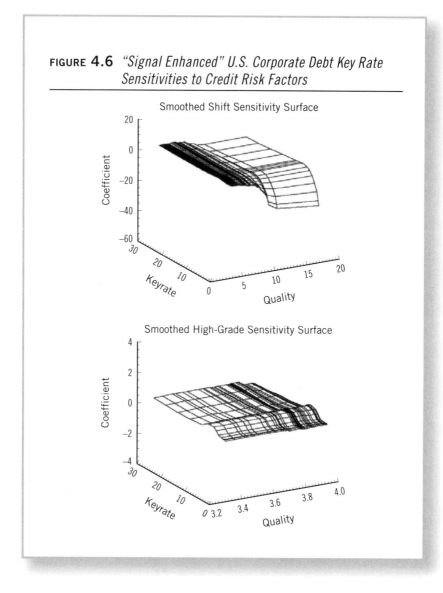

FIGURE **4.6** *"Signal Enhanced" U.S. Corporate Debt Key Rate Sensitivities to Credit Risk Factors*

These factors introduce significant "noise" to the underlying fundamental relationship. As shown in **FIGURE 4.6**, we used image recognition software with the objective of separating the "signal" from the noise (consistent with the primary objective of filtering out cosmic background noise from images transmitted from distant galaxies). The software has provided a clearer picture, and permitted us to develop a set of risk factor sensitivities with good explanatory power across which the relationships among sensitivities are extremely well behaved.

FIGURE **4.7** *Persistence of Credit Relationships*

Independent Spread Series	Industrial A, 5 Year	Industrial A, 5 Year
Dependent Spread Series	Industrial A, 1 Year	Industrial BB+, 5 Year
Average Beta	0.31	0.60
Minimum Beta	−0.24	0.23
Maximum Beta	0.88	0.91
Time-Shifted Correlation	0.15	0.01

In establishing the relationship between individual credits and risk factors, we wanted to determine if the shape of the credit sensitivity surfaces were dynamic or structural. In other words, we wanted to determine if forward risks should be measured using the relationships demonstrated in recent markets (which would be dynamic) or those demonstrated over the long term (which would be structural and static). In determining the answer to this question, we analyzed the persistence of the relationships across maturities and credit qualities. In particular, we analyzed the following relationships, which are detailed in **FIGURE 4.7**:

❏ The behavior of Industrial A credit spreads at the 1-year key rate relative to that at the 5-year key rate

❏ The behavior of Industrial BB+ credit spreads at the 5-year key rate relative to that of Industrial A spreads at the 5-year key rate

For both comparisons, we took the daily spread from 1991 to the present and calculated for each day the one-year rolling beta of the relationship. As is shown, the resulting beta in both cases varied dramatically over the fifteen-year time period. Finally, we calculated the correlation of the series of betas for each year versus the series of betas for the previous year. If there were persistence in this relationship, a high correlation would have identified this persistence. As shown in the "Time-Shifted Correlation" results, there was no persistence in behavior. The correlation for the first relationship was a paltry 0.15 and for the second 0.01. This implies that while there was significant variability in this behavior over time, there was virtually no tendency for recent behavior to be predictive of near-term future behavior. Consequently, we decided to utilize the long-term relationship.

FIGURE **4.8** *Correlation of Funds to Credit Style Index*

	MINIMUM	AVERAGE	MAXIMUM
Emerging market	−0.53	0.55	0.92
Convertible arbitrage	−0.08	0.57	0.76
Distressed debt	−0.27	0.54	0.87
High yield	−0.26	0.51	0.88
Direct lending	−0.46	0.41	0.92
Structured credit	0.17	0.46	0.94

FIGURE **4.9** *Correlation of Funds to Credit Style Index*

Since 2000						
	EMERGING MARKET	CONVERTIBLE ARBITRAGE	DISTRESSED DEBT	HIGH YIELD	DIRECT LENDING	STRUCTURED CREDIT
Emerging market	1.00					
Convertible arbitrage	0.13	1.00				
Distressed debt	0.69	0.35	1.00			
High yield	0.67	0.21	0.66	1.00		
Direct lending	−0.02	0.29	−0.14	−0.05	1.00	
Structured credit	0.04	0.18	0.26	−0.07	−0.10	1.00
Old strategies	0.82	0.38	0.84	0.66	−0.01	0.57
All combined	0.92	0.40	0.86	0.80	0.00	0.11

Correlations and Diversification

This section explores the correlations among credit funds and the diversification benefit achieved by combining credit funds with other hedge fund strategies and other asset classes. **FIGURE 4.8** shows the minimum, average, and maximum correlation of specific funds to their respective HFR style indexes (we have created indexes for direct lending and structured credit since none already existed), for each credit style. The correlations for each style are very similar, averaging 51%.

As shown in **FIGURE 4.9**, the returns of various credit strategies demonstrate a significant degree of correlation to one another. Emerging market debt, distressed debt and high yield are highly correlated. Convertible arbitrage is positively correlated with those strategies, but less so. Direct lending and structured credit both demonstrate slight correlations with convertible arbitrage, and structured credit shows a slight correlation with distressed debt as well. Otherwise they both demonstrate minimal to no correlation with the other credit strategies. The last two rows of Figure 4.9

FIGURE 4.10 *Correlation of Credit Style Indexes to Markets*

Since 2000

	EMERGING MARKET	CONVERTIBLE ARBITRAGE	DISTRESSED DEBT	HIGH YIELD	DIRECT LENDING	STRUCTURED CREDIT
HFR Composite	0.88	0.28	0.73	0.56	−0.04	0.07
S&P 500	0.69	0.07	0.43	0.39	−0.21	0.02
S&P Small Cap	0.72	0.13	0.55	0.49	−0.12	0.08
Lehman Intermediate Government	−0.21	0.08	−0.17	−0.30	0.14	0.04
Lehman Intermediate Credit	0.07	0.25	0.15	0.02	0.11	0.09
Credit Only	0.52	0.37	0.59	0.57	−0.01	0.12
DXY (Dollar)	−0.18	−0.07	−0.21	−0.22	−0.03	0.03
GSCI (Commodity)	0.04	0.06	−0.07	0.00	−0.01	−0.08

show the correlations of each strategy to indexes created from:

❏ "Old" credit strategies, the first four (shaded) credit strategies (emerging market, convertible arbitrage, distressed debt, and high yield)

❏ All credit strategies, the first four in addition to the two new strategies (direct lending and structured credit)

This generally shows the same relationships as the individual index comparisons, however, the levels of correlation are even stronger.

The correlations of the credit style indexes to various markets, shown in **FIGURE 4.10**, are consistent with the above conclusions. Emerging market, distressed debt, and high-yield strategies demonstrate the greatest amount of correlation, in particular to the hedge fund and equity indexes. All strategies but direct lending and structured credit show strong correlations to the "Credit Only" index, which is calculated as the performance of the Lehman Intermediate Credit Index less the Lehman Intermediate Government Index.

FIGURE 4.11 *Correlation of Credit Aggregate Indexes to Markets*

	Since 1990		Since 2000	
	OLD STRATEGIES	ALL CREDIT	OLD STRATEGIES	ALL CREDIT
HFR Composite	0.86	0.81	0.87	0.77
S&P 500	0.56	0.51	0.61	0.51
S&P Small Cap	0.66	0.62	0.69	0.61
Lehman Intermediate Government	−0.04	0.00	−0.21	−0.15
Lehman Intermediate Credit	0.18	0.20	0.13	0.16
Credit Only	0.52	0.50	0.65	0.60
DXY (Dollar)	0.14	0.15	−0.22	−0.20
GSCI (Commodity)	−0.02	−0.04	0.02	−0.02

FIGURE 4.11 presents the correlation of both the old credit strategies and all the credit strategies to the same market indexes. This analysis is presented for both the period beginning in 1990 and the period beginning in 2000. The most striking finding is that the HFR Composite Index explains approximately 80% of the behavior of all the credit indexes. The broad conclusion is that credit hedge funds are in general extremely correlated to other hedge funds. The second finding is that credit funds show significant correlation to the S&P 500, in particular they are highly correlated to the S&P Small Cap Index, which is not that surprising given that the HFR Composite Index has a 0.86 correlation to the S&P Small Cap Index. The third finding is that credit funds are relatively uncorrelated to the Lehman Intermediate U.S. Government/Credit Bond Index, the Dollar Index, and the Goldman Sachs Commodities Index (GSCI). The last finding is that credit hedge funds are strongly correlated to the Credit Only Index. The fact that credit hedge funds demonstrate this correlation while they show only limited correlation to the Lehman Intermediate Credit Index indicates that this index is actually dominated by interest rates, rather than credit spreads. Only after stripping the interest rate piece from the Lehman Intermediate Credit Index do we see correlation to the credit hedge funds.

Having identified small-cap equities and credit as the primary drivers of the performance of credit hedge funds, we can decompose the returns of these funds into beta (the component of returns that results from the behavior of the underlying markets) and alpha (the returns attributable to the

FIGURE 4.12 *Credit Hedge Fund Compound Annual Alpha by Style*

	2003	2004	2005	2006	2003–2005
Emerging market	14.75%	7.15%	12.41%	12.4%	11.6%
Convertible arbitrage	1.91%	−2.19%	−6.40%	4.2%	−0.7%
Distressed debt	16.60%	12.68%	6.48%	7.2%	10.7%
High yield	14.38%	7.36%	5.24%	8.2%	8.7%
Direct lending	12.54%	10.03%	10.37%	10.7%	10.9%
Structured credit	19.49%	16.33%	9.93%	9.4%	13.7%

fund's ability to outperform the underlying markets). **FIGURE 4.12** shows the results of this analysis by credit strategy. The broad conclusion is that a material part of the recent returns of credit hedge funds has been beta.

Portfolio Construction

The key to achieving a risk-efficient portfolio construction is proactively managing diversification. This is valid at the

- ❑ Security level
- ❑ Trade level
- ❑ Fund level
- ❑ Across all credit funds
- ❑ Across all hedge funds
- ❑ Across all alternative investments
- ❑ Across a full portfolio of both traditional and alternative investments.

We will again utilize Risk Fundamentals as an example of how this can be accomplished.

Risk Fundamentals uses the credit risk factors discussed earlier in conjunction with equity, interest rates, physical commodity, currency, and real estate risk factors to permit investors to aggregate risk across disparate holdings. As sensitivities to risk factors are additive across funds, providing a risk factor-based profile of a fund permits superior risk transparency. Risk Fundamentals permits funds to provide investors with risk transparency without requiring position disclosure. By applying this holistic risk factor framework, investors can construct a risk-efficient portfolio of investments.

Risk Fundamentals applies a "risk budgeting" framework to support the construction of a portfolio of funds. Risk budgeting is an approach developed and used by sophisticated institutional investors. In contrast to the traditional process of asset allocation, risk budgeting allocates risk. This methodology permits investors to achieve the ultimate goal of maximizing return per unit of risk, rather than the simpler goal of maximizing absolute return, which ignores the inherent risk in the underlying funds and the portfolio.

Risk Fundamentals permits investors to understand the correlations:

- ❑ Among funds
- ❑ Between each fund and the portfolio construction.

Furthermore, Risk Fundamentals' risk factor framework provides a fundamental understanding of the source of this correlation so that investors can proactively manage the construction of a portfolio.

The Risk Fundamentals portfolio construction module is based on the concept of marginal risk and marginal risk-adjusted returns. Marginal risk is the incremental risk resulting from adding an extremely small position to a portfolio construction. Marginal risk can be calculated as the product of the risk of the position (generally measured as standard deviation) and the correlation of that position to the portfolio. If the position has a correlation of 1, the incremental risk is completely additive and no diversification benefit is enjoyed. If the returns of the position are independent (correlation equals zero) of those of the portfolio, then adding the position will add no risk to the combined portfolio. If the returns of the position are negatively correlated to those of the portfolio, then adding the position actually represents a hedge, and the risk of the combined portfolio will be less than that of the original portfolio.

Marginal risk has several benefits. While risk is inherently amorphous, nonlinear, and nonadditive, marginal risk represents a well-behaved and additive framework. Furthermore, a fundamental understanding of marginal risk can be directly applied to the construction of a portfolio. By increasing investments in funds with low marginal risk and reducing investments in funds with high marginal risk, investors can deploy risk more efficiently. Finally, multiplying the size of each position times the marginal risk of that position results in a "risk contribution" that, across all holdings, sums to 100%. Therefore, risk contribution is an additive framework that comprehensively attributes the risk of a portfolio construction to each of the underlying holdings.

By extending this methodology to marginal risk-adjusted returns (marginal Sharpe ratio), Risk Fundamentals permits an investor to "optimize" the portfolio construction. We use the word *optimize* cautiously because, while a disciplined and rigorous quantitative analysis should be an important input to the portfolio construction process, the ultimate construction should be a judgmental decision that integrates both quantitative and qualitative factors. Marginal Sharpe combines returns, volatility, and correlations, thus, allowing the maximization of risk-adjusted returns. Marginal Sharpe measures the impact on the Sharpe ratio of a portfolio of adding a small increment of a position. Increasing holdings of positions with positive marginal Sharpe ratios improves the overall performance of the portfolio. Reducing holdings of positions with negative marginal Sharpe ratios also improves the overall performance of the portfolio.

When constructing any portfolio of investments, investors should be seeking to maximize idiosyncratic risk and minimize market risk. This is for two reasons:

1 Most investors have exposure to market risk (basic duration) through their traditional fixed income holdings.

2 Investors can gain access to market risk at fees significantly below those of hedge funds. Investors should be seeking funds that can generate alpha through security selection.

Thus, marginal risk plays a very important role here. As discussed previously, marginal risk provides a framework for investors to understand the risk contribution of an investment to a given portfolio. Using this framework, an investor can measure the amount of risk that each investment adds to the portfolio, and he or she can proactively manage the degree of idiosyncratic risk versus market risk within the portfolio.

A final portfolio construction question is how many different credit funds an investor should incorporate into a diversified portfolio of investments. The answer depends on the specific styles of the credit hedge funds being considered:

❑ For long-biased credit strategies making directional trades, such as distressed debt, emerging market and long-biased high-yield funds, selecting a relatively small number of superior funds creates the greatest value. The fundamental logic is that such funds are highly correlated, and, therefore, there are diminishing returns from increased diversification. Therefore, the greatest value is from selecting superior funds.

❑ For long-biased credit strategies making idiosyncratic trades, such as direct lending and structured credit funds, the more funds the better (assuming they are all of relatively equal quality). The fundamental logic is that such funds are relatively uncorrelated and diversifying across uncorrelated funds creates significant risk efficiencies.

❑ For long or short credit strategies making directional trades, in particular high-yield funds that take industry or geographic trades, selecting a relatively small number of superior funds creates the greatest value. The fundamental logic is that the greater the number of such funds the more likely that their directional plays are simply diversified away. Therefore, the greatest value is from selecting superior funds.

❑ For long or short credit strategies making relative value trades (for example, credit market neutral), such as duration neutral high-yield and convertible arbitrage funds, the more funds the better (assuming they are all of relatively equal quality). The fundamental logic is that such funds are relatively uncorrelated and diversifying across uncorrelated funds creates significant risk efficiencies.

Liquidity and Leverage

Another risk related to credit hedge funds is liquidity and the related issue of leverage. Leverage is related because it can be potentially required to fund losses during periods of illiquidity. Credit instruments broadly suffer from lower liquidity than equities, pure interest-rate instruments, or futures. Furthermore, many of the more complex securities used by hedge funds (for example, MBS derivatives, distressed debt, complex tranches of CDOs) are even less liquid than credit securities used by traditional managers (for example, investment grade corporate bonds, MBS collateral, high-grade CDOs). Finally, to the extent that specific credit strategies are long or short, hedge funds tend to go long the less liquid instruments and short the more liquid instruments (for example, distressed debt funds tend to go long nonperforming debt and hedge, with high-yield debt). This creates a significant basis risk in the event of a liquidity crunch.

While unleveraged funds can lose money, they cannot "blow up." The events of the fall of 1998 (LTCM/Russian default/MBS blowout) showed that mixing illiquidity and leverage can be explosive. These events have made both fund managers and investors woefully aware of the risk of illiquidity and the related risk of leverage. Funds have generally responded by reducing leverage and establishing lines of credit with terms that better match the liquidity of the underlying assets. In 1998, funds that were able to weather the storm generally recovered all or the vast majority of their losses within a couple of months. Only those that could not fund their losses through the depth of the crisis blew up. Since then, funds investing in illiquid instruments have generally reduced their leverage (although leverage has increased at other levels such as at the fund of funds). Furthermore, credit funds have attempted to establish longer-term financing including:

❑ Term repos (loans that are committed for two or three months)
❑ Evergreen financing (loans that automatically roll over)
❑ Long-term lines of credit

While these practices, on paper, should give investors a significantly greater level of comfort that funds can sustain a liquidity crunch, the agreements have generally been written with "force majeure" clauses that give lenders a way out in truly "extreme" circumstances. Both funds and, even more so, investors may be unpleasantly surprised when the next "hundred-year storm" hits. The key to avoiding blowups is matching the redemption and notice terms of the fund with the liquidity of the underlying holdings. In an attempt to do so, credit hedge funds have been generally extending their redemption and notice terms.

Investors should recognize that a fund can take on leverage without borrowing. Derivatives can result in significant leverage without requiring any borrowing. The demise of Amaranth represents a case of a fund enjoying hoards of cash experiencing a run on the bank as derivative trades went dramatically against them. As credit derivative strategies become increasingly complex and sophisticated, investors should beware of such potential risks. It is interesting that the size of the credit derivative market (particular the CDS market) is significantly larger than the size of the underlying market in cash credit securities (in contrast to the extremely large cash Treasury market, which underlies the interest-rate swap market). However, as the vast majority of credit derivatives can be settled in cash, the scarcity of underlying securities should not represent a problem in the market (the turnover of derivatives on many physical commodity markets is significantly greater than the turnover of the underlying physical market).

As illiquidity and leverage combined represent the fuse, Risk Fundamentals has introduced two measures that logically combine these factors: the "liquidity volatility" and the "redemption volatility." The liquidity volatility is the annualized standard deviation during the time that would be required for a manager to liquidate the portfolio. The liquidity volatility is calculated as the annualized standard deviation multiplied by the time-weighted (weighted by the square root of t) period it would take to liquidate each increment of the holdings. The redemption volatility is the annualized standard deviation during the time that would be required for an investor to liquidate his hedge fund holding (the sum of the length of the redemption cycle and the notice period).

An investor must ask whether to accept this liquidity risk. In asking this question, an investor must consider the fact that illiquid instruments earn a "liquidity premium." While it is impossible to isolate this piece of the return from the entire return stream, it is well recognized that illiquid investments "on average" (this is a key phrase) earn a premium to compensate them for this risk. If a liquidity event forced an investor to precipitously liquidate illiquid holdings, the left tail losses would likely more than offset the normal market compensation previously discussed.

Let's explore how best to measure the liquidity of credit funds. While Risk Fundamentals calculates the average daily turnover of exchange-traded securities (particularly equities) and uses this to measure the time it would take to liquidate a fund's holding of that security, this measure is not feasible for over-the-counter (OTC) markets because turnover data is not available. Furthermore, it is not clear that such a calculation represents a good measure of liquidity in these markets. While the exchange-traded markets tend to experience relatively frequent trading, the trading volumes on OTC markets tend to be lumpy. Just because there was a sizable trade in a 2014 IBM bond several days ago with no recent activity in the 2015 IBM bond does not mean that the 2014 bond trades more actively than the 2015 bond, which might have a large transaction in the near future. This lumpiness is even more accentuated across issuers. Despite the fact that the NASD-sponsored Trace reporting system has begun to provide information on the trading activities of many dollar-denominated corporate bonds, except for the most liquid issues, it is questionable how indicative this historical data is of the future liquidity of a specific issue. Furthermore, this data does not even exist for the majority of dollar-denominated credit instruments and is not available at all outside the United States.

Given this situation, how can investors best measure liquidity of credit securities? Risk Fundamentals has employed a simple but elegant solution proposed by Verne Sedlacek, CEO of the Commonfund. The concept behind this solution is that it is more important to create a standard measurement of liquidity that is consistently applied across funds, than it is to establish a precise measure of liquidity (which frankly is not feasible). The solution establishes reasonable standard measures of the liquidity of different types of securities (for example, on-the-run Treasuries, off-the-run Treasuries, MBS collateral, agency derivatives, nonagency derivatives). These measures are based on the consensus judgment of experienced market participants. Consistently applying these standards across hedge funds provides a very valuable measure of relative liquidity, if not an exact measure of absolute liquidity. In equities, it is reasonable to assume that the larger the holding of a stock the longer it will take to liquidate. This is not true in the bond markets. Bond positions generally have a minimum size below which liquidating the holding actually becomes more difficult. Subscale holdings are appropriately called "odd lots."

Thus, OTC security liquidity is undoubtedly the one measure of risk that is least accurately represented. The vast majority of funds claim to be able to liquidate all their holdings in a fraction of the time actually required to do so without adversely impacting the realized price, but, because there has been no way to measure this, investors have had to accept these claims at face value (knowing that they are exaggerations). However, if all hedge funds uniformly applied the same set of standards and provided portfolio-level aggregations of liquidity, the resulting measures would be extremely valuable for comparing liquidity across funds. Investors would no longer have to live with exaggerated liquidity claims.

It is important to note that these standard liquidity assumptions have been created based on "normal" markets. Liquidity really becomes a significant issue in "crisis" markets. However, experience in such markets is inadequate to meaningfully impute "norms" under crisis conditions.

Therefore, we have made the assumption that the general relationship across assets would be elongated but would remain relatively consistent across different types of assets under such conditions.

Valuation

An issue related to illiquidity is valuation. How accurate are the NAVs of credit funds?

It is difficult to precisely value anything but the most liquid instruments. One might attribute the problem to the fact that all credit instruments are traded OTC. However, Treasuries and currencies are both OTC instruments in which the underlying markets are so liquid that they permit price discovery that equals that of exchange-traded equities and is significantly better than exchange-traded options. The issue of valuation is not one of exchange versus OTC but rather of market liquidity.

While we have earlier argued that liquidity risk is appropriately compensated in the returns of illiquid securities, valuation risk is not. Again, we cannot isolate this risk and explicitly demonstrate this. Rather, this conclusion is based on the general belief that market risk is compensated and operation risk, of which valuation risk is a component, is not. Therefore, investors must diligently mitigate operational risk for which they are not rewarded. Operational risk often comes with the territory and cannot be completely avoided.

The key challenge in gaining comfort with a fund's NAV is removing any discretion from the manager. Valuation of illiquid instruments can never be "precise." Because these instruments are illiquid, they are not actively trading on a real-time basis and, therefore, price discovery does not permit an exact valuation. The degree to which this is the case ranges from slightly illiquid securities that may trade almost daily but not actively every second of the day to ones that trade "by appointment only."

Despite the fact that an investor must accept that valution is not precise, an investor has every right to expect that this imprecise process is unbiased. Investors should expect that NAVs be based on fair and independent valuations. The independence should require that the ultimate valuation be done by a third party and that the fund have no discretion over this valuation. Against this backdrop, the following disciplines should be followed:

❑ Where feasible, a third-party pricing source (for example, IDC, LPC) should be used. This ensures that the fund is using the same standard valuation as other funds holding the same security. If a fund disagrees with the valuation of any security, the fund should ask the third-party source to reevaluate the valuation. This enforces the discipline of uniformity of valuation across funds because if the source changes the valuation, it will be changed for all funds. If the third-party source concludes that its initial valuation is correct, the fund should not have the discretion to deviate from the source.

❑ The fund should push the third-party pricing source to cover as many securities that are held by the fund as possible (third-party sources will generally add coverage on request).

❑ For holdings that must be valued based on dealer quotes, the fund should identify the best brokers for specific (especially difficult to value) securities, but the administrator should be exclusively responsible for soliciting and processing the quotes. The fund should not have any discretion with respect to rejecting outlying quotes. The administrator should have the sole responsibility of deciding when to ask a broker to reevaluate a quote or to solicit additional quotes when there are significant differences among initial quotes.

❑ For holdings that must be valued at fair value, the fund should periodically utilize a third-party service that will make an independent valuation of that holding. Administrators do not provide an independent third-party valuation.

Beyond making investors question the validity of a credit fund's reported NAV, the imprecise valuation process for many credit securities can have a more pernicious impact on an investor's ability to understand the risk-adjusted returns of a credit hedge fund. Because of the muting of volatility, funds in our credit universe have an average Sharpe ratio of 2.2. This compares with an average across the broad hedge fund universe (Hedge Fund Research or HFR database) of 0.8. How should an investor think about this? While the real return behavior of credit hedge funds has been excellent, the reported performance significantly overstates the attractiveness of their risk-adjusted returns. The inflation is so great that if an investor were to optimize a portfolio that included the composite track record for the universe of credit funds and all the HFR indexes, the majority of the allocation to hedge funds would be directed to credit hedge funds. While this looks great, it is not real. Investors must recognize this and temper their enthusiasm. It is clear that some "adjustment" is required, but the question is how much. While there is no "precise" method to adjust smoothed returns, there is a rough method that enhances the informational content. The solution recognizes that smoothing returns introduces serial correlation to a return series. Regressing a return series by the same series time-shifted by one period provides a model to estimate what the returns may have been had the smoothing not occurred, thereby providing a series of returns that roughly adjusts for the smoothing.

Furthermore, the risk-factor framework previously discussed provides a valuable complement in understanding the true underlying volatility of a fund whose returns have been smoothed. The portfolio-level volatility calculated within the framework is based on the actual behavior of the underlying securities. Thus, the measured volatility is not dampened by the funds' valuation practices. Therefore, while risk factors do not solve the valuation challenge, they do permit an investor to gain a reasonably good fundamental understanding of the risk of the underlying portfolio without the artificial muting of return volatility introduced by the valuation process.

Sustainability and Scalability

After initial strong performance, the forward-looking question for credit strategies is whether this performance is repeatable. The general decline in returns over the past few years could lead one to question both the sustainability and scalability of this strategy.

As we have already stated, investors recognize that credit spreads in today's market are extremely narrow. Therefore, investors question whether the strong trailing performance of credit funds is because they fundamentally have an ability to generate alpha or rather because they have had the wind at their backs.

The issue of scalability is even more complex. Many credit funds recognize that being small and nimble is critical to their strategy and have established relatively low capacity limits. Furthermore, many funds have actually extended their redemption and notice terms, reflecting the relatively low liquidity of many of the underlying credit securities. This has reduced the percentage of available funds that are acceptable to investors who have established maximum redemption and notice period limits.

A textbook example of the issue of sustainability and scalability is convertible arbitrage. In the eight years of 1995 through 2002 convertible arbitrage funds generated a compound annual return of 13.3%. We have already shown in Figure 4.2 that since the beginning of 2003 convertible arbitrage has generated a compound annual return of 5.2%, approximately the risk-free rate during this period. What happened? Assets under management of convertible arbitrage funds grew by an order of magnitude between the beginning of 1995 and the beginning of 2003. Although estimates varied significantly, up to 80% of new convertible issues (the most conservative estimates place this at 40%) were purchased by, and up to 95% of convertibles bonds were traded by, hedge funds. Essentially, convertible arbitrage hedge funds became the market, and returns became a zero-sum game. In this particular strategy, returns proved to be neither sustainable nor scalable.

While the credit markets are extremely large, many credit funds pursue niche strategies. Across the hedge fund industry, there is a lot of money chasing a declining set of opportunities. While attractive opportunities still exist in the credit markets, the number of hedge funds pursuing them is significantly greater than in earlier waves of alternative investments and, therefore, investors must continually be questioning the sustainability of the opportunity set.

Chapter Notes

1. The Risk Fundamentals System is owned by Risk Fundamentals LLC, of which Richard Horwitz is a principal.

PART TWO

Risk Management Strategies

CHAPTER 5

Risk Management of Credit Derivatives

SANTA FEDERICO, ANDREA PETRELLI,
JUN ZHANG, AND VIVEK KAPOOR

R isk management of credit derivatives poses special challenges: credit derivatives confront all the same issues as more traditional credit instruments, such as corporate bonds and loans. However, credit derivatives are also exposed to the gamut of exotic risks—delta, gamma, correlation, and others, that challenge derivatives risk management everywhere. Further, the interaction of credit and market risk presents further challenges to those working with credit derivatives, not to mention a whole new vocabulary of terms, such as *senior/subordinate tranches*, *copula functions*, and *base correlation*.

The purpose of this chapter is to remove some of the mystery surrounding the terminology used by practitioners in the field of credit derivatives risk management, and to illustrate the risks of credit derivatives with concrete examples. To this end, sample transactions using credit default swaps (CDS) and synthetic collateralized debt obligations (CDO) have been chosen because of their illustrative ability as well as their current popularity in the marketplace.

A Lexicon of Risks

The focus of this discussion is on those risks that are traditionally characterized as credit or market risks: credit or default risk is the risk that an obligor fails to fully meet financial obligations. Examples include the risk that an obligor or its bond defaults, that a coupon payment may be missed, that debt may need to be restructured, or that a derivative counterparty fails to make its promised payments. These are the types of risks that credit derivatives are designed to mitigate.

Market risks are those risks that affect the market value of a financial transaction. These include the traditional risks, such as interest-rate risk, credit-spread risk, foreign-exchange risk, equity price risk, and others, as well as the more exotic derivatives-type risks, such as volatility risk, correlation risk, and so on. While these risks are traditionally the purview of other derivative products, the creativity of credit derivative structures has opened the door for these risks as well.

To be sure, other types of risks play an important role in the management of credit derivatives. These include legal risk, operational risk, liquidity risk, and so on. Indeed, many of the largest losses in the financial industry in recent history can be attributed to these types of risks. However, as often said when one cannot or does not want to talk about them, these risks are beyond the scope of this presentation.

Single-Name Credit Default Swap

Description

A CDS transfers the credit risk of a reference entity from one party to another. **FIGURE 5.1** illustrates a typical credit default swap:

Suppose the protection buyer purchases protection for the Ford Motor Company by paying a premium of 100 bps per year. The total notional of the transaction is $100 mm and the maturity is five years. In this example, the protection buyer purchases protection on the possibility of $100 mm debt defaulting over a five-year period from the protection seller. For this insurance, the buyer pays the protection seller an annual premium of $100 mm × 100 bps, which is $1 mm, paid in quarterly installments. This

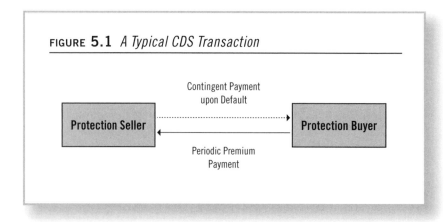

FIGURE **5.1** *A Typical CDS Transaction*

premium is referred to as the CDS coupon or deal spread. In the event of default, the protection buyer receives a payment equal to the loss amount that will be notional $\times$ (1 $-$ recovery). If we *assume* the recovery is 30%, then the payment from the protection seller will be $100 mm $\times$ (1 $-$ 0.3), which is $70 mm.

In the following discussion, different types of risk associated with the CDS are presented. The key concepts behind CDS valuations are presented in Chapter 9, which presents analytical results for valuation and risk sensitivities under idealized conditions. The details of the sample sensitivities are shown next.

Default Risk

The default risk associated with the possibility of Ford defaulting is borne by the protection seller. Assuming a recovery of 30%, in the event of default, the protection seller is obligated to make a payment of $70 mm to the protection buyer and, as such, represents the credit risk of the transaction.[1]

One complication that impacts the determination of default risk is the fact that the payment that the protection seller makes to the protection buyer in the event of default is not necessarily known in advance. Recovery and the default event timing are both unknown random quantities at the time of entering a CDS.

CDSs can be either physically or cash settled. In a physically settled CDS, upon default the protection buyer delivers the reference obligation (or the cheapest bond from an agreed upon basket) to the protection seller who pays the par amount to the protection buyer. Similarly, cash-settled CDSs compensate the protection buyer in the event of default by having the protection seller pay the protection buyer a loss amount due to the default based on a default price established by a dealer poll. Both these settlement mechanisms have floating/uncertain recovery values associated with them. In a relatively small fraction of default-swap contracts, the recovery percentage is fixed (for example, 50%): these are referred to as digital default swaps (DDS). It's only in this last case that the default contingent payment is known with certainty. However, purchasing DDS protection does not hedge a long position in a bond like a CDS because the recovery in the event of default is not known. Similarly, selling DDS protection and purchasing CDS protection entails recovery risk.

A useful concept to introduce here is that of value on default (VOD). VOD measures the change in the mark-to-market value of the transaction due to the event of sudden default. When a default occurs, two things happen: the CDS is terminated and, therefore, any positive or negative mark-to-market value to either the buyer or seller of protection is extinguished.

The protection seller is also obligated to compensate the protection buyer for the default in one of the manners described previously. Therefore, the VOD is the sum of two quantities, the current mark-to-market and default settlement payment.

To illustrate the VOD concept, let's continue with the Ford example. Assuming that CDS spreads have widened by 100 bps since the inception of the transaction, the mark-to-market value of the transaction to the protection seller and buyer will be –$4.28 mm and $4.28 mm, respectively (Chapter 9 presents details and idealizations that are behind the example shown here). Upon default, the protection seller must make a payment of $70 mm to the protection buyer (based on assumed recovery fraction of 0.3). The VOD to the protection seller and buyer could then be calculated as –$70 mm + $4.28 mm (–$65.72 mm) and $70 mm – $4.24 mm ($65.72 mm), respectively. This VOD is uncertain insofar as the actual recovery is different from 30%, the payout upon default will be different from a VOD calculated assuming 30% recovery. A VOD can also be assessed by setting the CDS spreads to some very high number and taking the mark-to-market change after the credit spread jumps.

At this point, the reader may be wondering why no mention has been made of the other risks that typically affect derivatives transactions, such as volatility risk. After all, a credit default swap has a certain option-like character in that the cash flows between the protection buyer and seller are contingent upon a certain event (that is, default). This looks like a knock-in or binary option. Why then are these other derivatives risks not involved?

The answer is that the traditional paradigm used for the valuation of credit derivatives is based on a reduced-form modeling framework (Jarrow and Turnbull, 1995). In this framework, all the information necessary to value a CDS is embedded in market CDS spreads and interest rates. No fundamental information of the company in question, its balance sheet, probability of default, and so forth, is incorporated. This is in contrast to structural modeling approaches, which are based on the Merton model for corporate debt that explicitly incorporates this type of information (Merton, 1974). However, the risk-neutral valuation of a CDS in the reduced-form framework, per se, does not result in a quantification of the real-world default probability. Among the sources of real-world default probabilities are (1) rating agencies, (2) structural model vendors like KMV, and (3) hybrid structural-econometric models (for example, Kamakura).

Market Risk

There are primarily two market risks associated with this transaction: credit-spread risk and interest-rate risk. Credit-spread risk dominates over the interest-rate risk in the market risk of the CDS transaction.

Credit-Spread Risk

The credit-spread risk associated with a CDS arises due to the possibility that market CDS spreads may change, thereby affecting its mark-to-market value. A seller of protection has similar economic exposure to a bondholder (they are both "long" credit) as both parties are adversely affected by spread widening. The converse is true for the protection buyer. This risk is typically measured by using static sensitivity measures such as CS01 (that is, the impact of a 1 basis-point [bp] increase in credit spreads on the value of the transaction). Chapter 9 illustrates analytic details and presents some examples for CS01 calculation. For the example above, the CS01 for protection seller is –$44.3 K. In other words, the protection seller would lose $44.3 K if Ford's credit spread widened from 100 to 101 bps. Note that there is some "convexity" associated with the credit-spread risk. If the CDS spread widens from 100 to 200 bps, this 100 bps widening will result in a $4.28 mm decrease in the transaction's market value for protection seller, which is somewhat less than 100 times the CS01.

Interest-Rate Risk

The valuation of a CDS is also affected by changes in the level of interest rates. The impact, however, is generally minimal and only becomes nonzero when the credit spread moves away from the original spread. In this example, if we assume the credit spread widened to 200 bps in one year, a 1 bp increase in interest rates results in a mark-to-market gain of $101 K to the protection seller. The DV01 is the change in mark-to-market in response to interest rates rising by 1 bp. The reason for the positive DV01 in this example is because the loss amount due to credit-spread widening is reduced by a higher discount rate. Refer to Chapter 9 for details of the DV01 calculation.

Synthetic CDO

Description

In recent years, synthetic collateralized debt obligations (CDO) have proliferated. A synthetic CDO can be tailored to the risk appetites of different classes of investors. **FIGURE 5.2** shows the typical synthetic CDO structure. The lower strike (or "attachment point") is where cumulative loss experience begins to impair the tranche, and the upper strike (or "detachment point") is where the tranche is wiped out and unable to absorb further losses. The equity tranche absorbs the first loss in the reference pool (for example, the first 3%). The next ("mezzanine") tranche absorbs losses in the reference pool beginning at the equity tranche's upper strike and up to the mezzanine's upper strike.

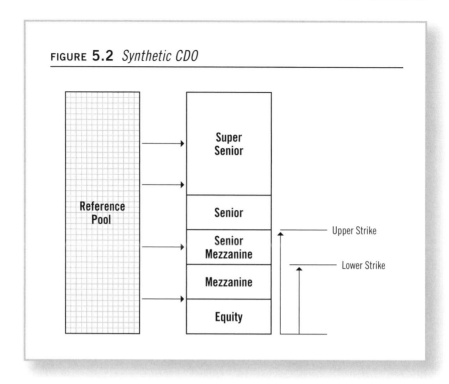

FIGURE **5.2** *Synthetic CDO*

TABLE **5.1** *Quotes on CDX.NA.IG.4 for March 31, 2005*

CDX.NA.IG.4—6/20/10—Ref 49—Assumes Delta Exchange

TRANCHE	DESC	INDICATIVE BID	OFFER	CORR (MID)	DELTA	AXE (PROT)
0–3%	Equity	500+33.00%	500+34.00%	19%	17.0x	B/S
3–7%	BBB-	195	203	5%	7.0x	B/S
7–10%	AAA	61	67	16%	2.8x	B/S
10–15%	AAA+	23	27	21%	1.1x	B/S
15–30%	Super Sen.	8	12	32%	0.3x	B/S

Quotes on tranches referencing credit indexes, such as CDX.NA.IG. (which is described later), are widely available on a daily frequency. Table 5.1 presents the quotes of CDX.NA.IG.4 for March 31, 2005. To under-

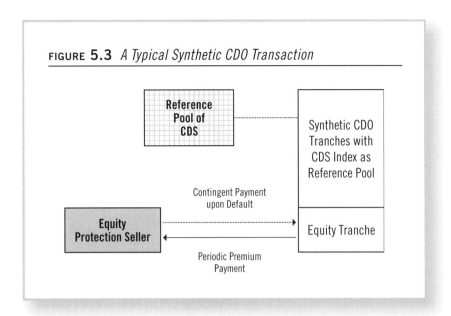

FIGURE **5.3** *A Typical Synthetic CDO Transaction*

stand the quotes in the table, let's look at quotes for the equity tranche. Table 5.1 shows that the dealer is willing to pay 500 bps/yr running and an up-front payment of 33% of the tranche notional to buy credit protection in the 0% to 3% region. The corresponding implied correlation from the CDO pricing model is 19%. While the equity tranche in the quote shown in **TABLE 5.1** trades on a mix of fixed running (500 bps/yr) and up-front, the other tranches trade on running spread.

A protection seller has to make whole the protection buyer for any default losses in the reference pool that exceed the tranche lower strike, until the losses exceed the upper strike. The tranche notional is the original notional minus the amount by which the reference pool losses have exceeded the lower strike—with a floor at zero. The instant the pool losses exceed the tranche upper strike, the tranche notional becomes zero and subsequent default events do not result in any cash flow from the tranche protection seller to protection purchaser. In return, the protection purchaser has to pay the protection seller a combination of up-front payments and periodic payments based on the tranche premium rate multiplied by the outstanding tranche notional.

Again, we will use a detailed example of a synthetic CDO to illustrate the major concepts and the mechanisms of the transaction. **FIGURE 5.3** shows a typical synthetic CDO equity tranche transaction, where the investor sold protection on the equity tranche. Suppose the underlying reference pool includes 100 names, and each name has a notional of $1 mm and recovery of 30%.

So the total notional for the pool will be $100 mm. Let's also assume that the investor or the protection seller sells protection on the equity tranche (0% to 3%) with the running premium of 500 bps for five years and an up-front payment of 40% of tranche notional. In this case, the dollar amount of the lower attachment is $0, the upper detachment is $3 mm and the tranche notional is $3 mm. The protection seller will receive an up-front payment of $3 mm × 40% which is $1.2 mm, and an annual premium of $3 mm × 500 bps, which is $0.15 mm paid in quarterly installments. On the contingent payment side, the protection seller might need to pay the protection buyer in case of defaults, depending on whether the loss amount exceeds the lower strike. **TABLE 5.2** shows the loss mechanism for the 0% to 3% equity tranche protection seller as names in the pool default. When a name defaults, the defaulted name will be removed from the pool, and the pool notional will be reduced by the notional of the defaulted name. More specifically, the equity tranche notional will be reduced by defaulted name notional × (1 − recovery), and

TABLE 5.2 *Loss Mechanism of the 0% to 3% of Equity Tranche Protection Seller*

NUMBER OF NAMES DEFAULTED	POOL NOTIONAL ($MM)	LOWER STRIKE ($MM)	UPPER STRIKE ($MM)	EACH PAYMENT MADE BY PROTECTION SELLER ($MM)	CUMULATIVE PAYMENT MADE BY PROTECTION SELLER ($MM)
0	100	0	3.0	0	0
1	99	0	2.3	0.7	0.7
2	98	0	1.6	0.7	1.4
3	97	0	0.9	0.7	2.1
4	96	0	0.2	0.7	2.8
5	95	0	0	0.2	3
6	94	0	0	0	3
7	93	0	0	0	3
8	92	0	0	0	3
9	91	0	0	0	3
10	90	0	0	0	3

the super senior tranche will be reduced by the amount of defaulted name notional × recovery. This mechanism ensures that the pool notional and the total possible tranche protection notional are matched.

A popular type of CDS pool is in the form of the credit indexes, which are standard pools of credits that trade in a group, similar to equity indexes. These indexes are equally weighted (that is, each credit has the same notional size). The index market has grown rapidly and is now very liquid, with standard quotes of $100 mm with a 1 bp bid-ask spread. Indexes cover the full yield curve (three-month, six-month, one-year, two-year, and so on), although five-year point is most liquid. One of the most popular indexes is the CDX North American Investment Grade Index (CDX.NA.IG). This index consists of 125 reference obligors. The value of the index is based on the five-year CDS spreads of the individual obligors. As of March 31, 2005, the five-year spread of this index was 49 bps. **FIGURES 5.4** and **5.5** illustrate the composition of this popular credit index (series 4), and **TABLE 5.3** gives a partial list of the names in the order of decreasing credit spreads.

Similar to the risk in CDS, synthetic CDOs also have default risk and market risks. The difference is that, in the market risk of synthetic CDOs, there is an additional risk: correlation risk. Both the default risk and the market risks are discussed next. The example presented here to illustrate different risks is based on March 31, 2005, CDX.NA.IG.4 (that is, the

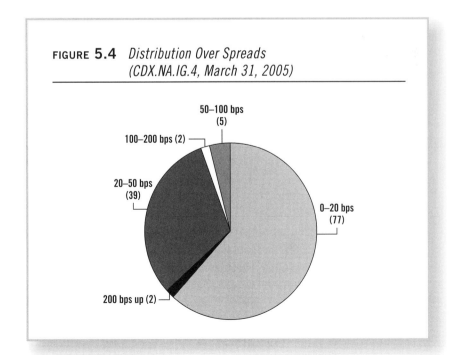

FIGURE 5.4 *Distribution Over Spreads (CDX.NA.IG.4, March 31, 2005)*

50–100 bps (5)

100–200 bps (2)

20–50 bps (39)

200 bps up (2)

0–20 bps (77)

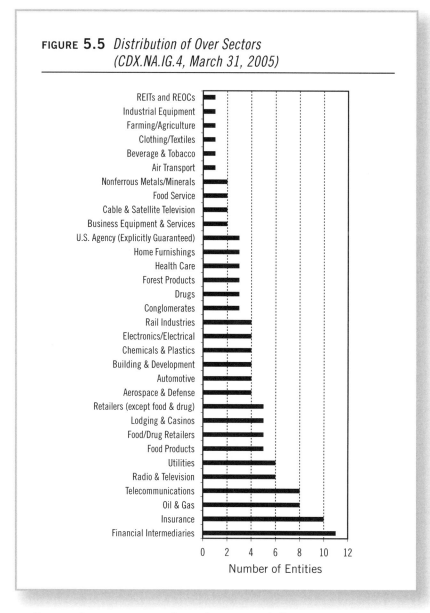

FIGURE 5.5 *Distribution of Over Sectors (CDX.NA.IG.4, March 31, 2005)*

credit spread term structure for each name and discount rate curve are all based on March 31, 2005). The recovery is assumed to be 30% for each name. We focus on the equity tranche to illustrate risk sensitivities. The equity tranche is quoted in terms of a fixed running premium (500 bps) and a bid-offer on up-front payment. The synthetic CDO analytic model to illustrate risk sensitivities follows the standard market practice and is described in Chapter 10.

TABLE 5.3 *Top 25 Names by Credit Spreads (CDX.NA.IG.4, March 31, 2005)*

OBLIGOR	5-YEAR SPREAD (BPS)
General Motors Acceptance Corporation	456
Ford Motor Credit Company	281
American Axle & Manufacturing Inc.	277
Maytag Corporation	200
Liberty Media Corporation	151
Lear Corporation	143
Eastman Kodak Company	134
Sears Roebuck Acceptance Corporation	115
Autozone, Inc.	100
Clear Channel Communications, Inc.	93
Pulte Homes, Inc.	84
Kerr–McGee Corporation	84
Altria Group, Inc.	84
Arrow Electronics, Inc.	81
Centurytel, Inc.	81
Lennar Corporation	77
Cox Communications, Inc.	71
Albertson's, Inc.	69
Safeway Inc.	68
Centex Corporation	66
Mckesson Corporation	65
Jones Apparel Group, Inc.	65
Hilton Hotels Corporation	63
Cardinal Health, Inc.	63
Harrah's Operating Company, Inc.	62

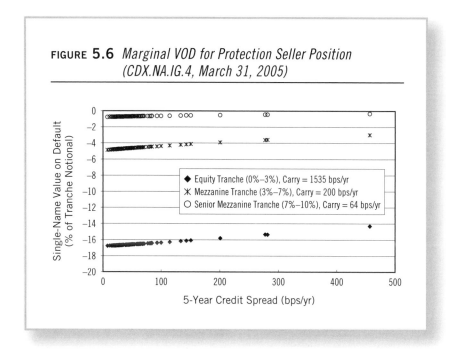

FIGURE **5.6** *Marginal VOD for Protection Seller Position (CDX.NA.IG.4, March 31, 2005)*

Default Risk

Similar to the single-name CDS, a synthetic CDO also has the default risk. When a default hits the tranche (that is, the pool losses lie within a tranche), the tranche protection seller will make a payment. However, the default risk in synthetic CDOs is more complicated than the single-name CDS. In the synthetic CDO world, the default risk not only refers to a single-name defaulting, but can also include multiple defaults (depending on tranche thickness and the sizes of the individual losses). In contrast, a CDS contract terminates when the reference issuer defaults.

Marginal Value on Default (VOD)

The default risk of the synthetic CDO can be characterized in a number of ways. The first is by the marginal VOD, or individual VOD of each obligor. The marginal VOD is defined as the change of the tranche mark-to-market due to the obligor defaulting. For example, a protection seller of 3% to 7% tranche will have a loss or negative VOD if one name defaults, even though one doesn't make any payment to the protection purchaser on the first default. This is because the mezzanine tranche on which one sold protection now has a smaller cushion and becomes more risky. All else being equal, the fair premium for this tranche postdefault should be higher than the original premium, which implies a mark-to-market loss for the protection seller. For the example of the CDX.NA.IG.4 mentioned above,

TABLE 5.4 *Top 25 Names of Running VOD for Equity Tranche Protection Seller (CDX.NA.IG.4, March 31, 2005)*

OBLIGOR	5-YEAR SPREAD (BPS)	VOD (% OF TRANCHE NOTIONAL)		
		CUMULATIVE CONTINGENT PAYMENT	CUMULATIVE MTM CHANGE	RUNNING VOD
General Motors Acceptance Corporation	456	−18.7%	4.4%	−14.3%
Ford Motor Credit Company	281	−37.3%	8.5%	−28.8%
American Axle & Manufacturing Inc.	277	−56.0%	14.0%	−42.0%
Maytag Corporation	200	−74.7%	21.2%	−53.5%
Liberty Media Corporation	151	−93.9%	32.0%	−61.9%
Lear Corporation	143	−100.0%	35.5%	−64.5%
Eastman Kodak Company	134	−100.0%	35.5%	−64.5%
Sears Roebuck Acceptance Corporation	115	−100.0%	35.5%	−64.5%
Autozone, Inc.	100	−100.0%	35.5%	−64.5%
Clear Channel Communications, Inc.	93	−100.0%	35.5%	−64.5%
Pulte Homes, Inc.	84	−100.0%	35.5%	−64.5%
Kerr−McGee Corporation	84	−100.0%	35.5%	−64.5%
Altria Group, Inc.	84	−100.0%	35.5%	−64.5%
Arrow Electronics, Inc.	81	−100.0%	35.5%	−64.5%
Centurytel, Inc.	81	−100.0%	35.5%	−64.5%
Lennar Corporation	77	−100.0%	35.5%	−64.5%
Cox Communications, Inc.	71	−100.0%	35.5%	−64.5%
Albertson's, Inc.	69	−100.0%	35.5%	−64.5%
Safeway Inc.	68	−100.0%	35.5%	−64.5%
Centex Corporation	66	−100.0%	35.5%	−64.5%
Mckesson Corporation	65	−100.0%	35.5%	−64.5%
Jones Apparel Group, Inc.	65	−100.0%	35.5%	−64.5%
Hilton Hotels Corporation	63	−100.0%	35.5%	−64.5%
Cardinal Health, Inc.	63	−100.0%	35.5%	−64.5%
Harrah's Operating Company, Inc.	62	−100.0%	35.5%	−64.5%

the marginal VOD associated with the obligors for different tranches is illustrated in **FIGURE 5.6**. The marginal VOD for each tranche is relatively uniform because each name has the same notional weight in the index.

The marginal VOD is a good measurement of default risk for the synthetic CDOs, but it only gives the VOD of each obligor defaulting in isolation and does not tell us much about the VOD associated with multiple simultaneous defaults. One way to characterize the impact of multiple defaults simultaneously is through the cumulative or running VOD.

Running Value on Default (VOD)

The running VOD associated with N number of defaults is calculated by ordering the obligors by decreasing CDS spreads as per Table 5.3, and simultaneously defaulting N number of obligors in this order. Ordering the names as such provides an easily interpreted measure of aggregate credit risk: the greater the CDS spread, the greater the market implied probability of default. As N increases, more of the higher quality credits default, implying an incremental deterioration in the credit environment that affects that basket. For the equity tranche protection seller, the running VODs associated with the obligors in Table 5.3 are illustrated in **TABLE 5.4**. Table 5.4 shows, for example, that if GMAC defaults, the 0%–3% protection seller will lose 14.3% of the tranche notional where the contingent payment is –18.7% and the mark-to-market is 4.4%; if

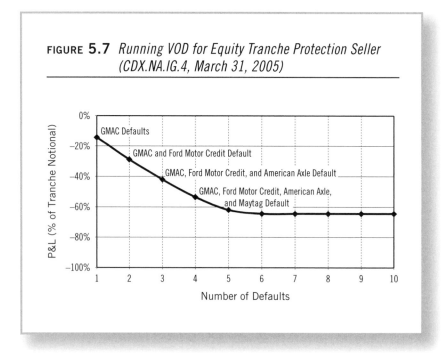

FIGURE **5.7** *Running VOD for Equity Tranche Protection Seller (CDX.NA.IG.4, March 31, 2005)*

both GMAC and Ford Motor Credit default, the protection seller will lose 28.8% of tranche notional; if GMAC, Ford Motor Credit, and American Axle all default, the protection seller will lose 42% of tranche notional and so forth. The loss amount is bounded above by the thickness of the tranche, minus the up-front payment. In this example, the up-front payment received for selling protection on the equity tranche is 35%—hence a maximum loss amount of 65% of tranche notional.

In subsequent analyses, it will be useful to view the running VODs as a graph of the VOD versus number of defaulting obligors. Table 5.4 can be graphed as shown in **FIGURE 5.7**.

While running VOD is certainly a step in the right direction in terms of understanding the aggregate default risk of a portfolio of obligors, it does not provide any understanding as to the probability of any particular default scenario. By ordering names in decreasing order of credit spreads, we are getting insight into the expected default scenario (that is, weaker credits defaulting prior to stronger ones). This, however, does not address other possible default scenarios. To fully assess a portfolio's

TABLE 5.5 *Probability Distribution of Defaults Assuming 25% Asset Correlation (CDX.NA.IG.4, March 31, 2005)*

NUMBER OF DEFAULTS (n)	PROBABILITY OF n DEFAULTS	PROBABILITY OF LESS THAN OR EQUAL TO n DEFAULTS
0	85.07%	85.07%
1	10.35%	95.42%
2	2.65%	98.07%
3	0.93%	98.99%
4	0.47%	99.46%
5	0.23%	99.69%
6	0.13%	99.81%
7	0.06%	99.88%
8	0.06%	99.97%
9	0.02%	99.95%
10	0.01%	99.97%

aggregate default risk, it is necessary to consider the various possible default scenarios and the likelihood of each occurring.

One-Year VOD Distribution

The probability distribution of VOD is found via MC simulation. The way to perform this analysis is to simulate the time-to-default for each obligor in the pool and record those having a time-to-default less than one year. This simulation is performed employing the standard normal copula approach (see Chapter 10). The tranche is then reevaluated, and the mark-to-market change will be the VOD associated with this particular realization. A distribution of the VOD could be obtained by repeating the process many times. The VOD distribution over a one-year time horizon was calculated using 25% flat asset correlation for all the names in the pool and 50,000 simulation paths whose default probabilities were assigned using Standard & Poor's corporate default statistics (rating based). Alternatives to this approach include employing KMV and/or Kamakura default probabilities that are based on variants and extensions of the Merton model. Indeed, a proprietary view on default probabilities can be used. Be aware that the 25% correlation is used to simulate the time-to-default, while the market implied correlation is used to valuate each tranche. Obligor-pair specific correlations can also be used to simulate default events, and more sophisticated representations of the implied correlations can also be employed. **TABLE 5.5** shows the probability distribution of the number of name defaults.

FIGURES 5.8 and **5.9** demonstrate the results of MC simulation for one-year VOD distribution for CDX.NA.IG.4. Figure 5.8 shows the histogram of the one-year VOD distribution, which gives the probability of different VODs. The graph is discrete because each default event is discrete. For example, Figure 5.8 shows that there is an 85% chance of VOD taking a value of zero, which is because there is an 85% chance of no default within the next year. Figure 5.9 illustrates the one-year cumulative VOD distribution. From Figure 5.9, a "default VaR" can be derived. For example, Figure 5.9 shows that over a one-year horizon there is a 1% chance of losing more than 45% of equity tranche notional and, as such, represents a 99% confidence default VaR. This is a useful quantity for economic risk capital calculations.

The "default VaR" calculation shown above, incidentally, brings to bear another risk factor, namely, default correlation. To perform an MC simulation, it is necessary to make certain assumptions regarding the interdependency of the simulation paths. As stated above, the paths were simulated assuming a normal copula with 25% asset correlation. Changing this assumption to, for example, 30% correlation would result in the 99% confidence VaR increasing to 55% of equity tranche notional.

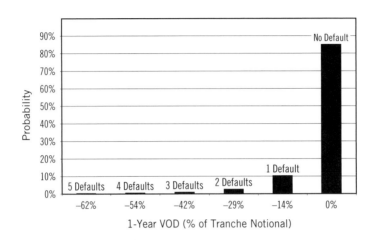

FIGURE **5.8** *One-Year VOD Histogram of Selling Equity Tranche Protection (CDX.NA.IG.4, March 31, 2005)*

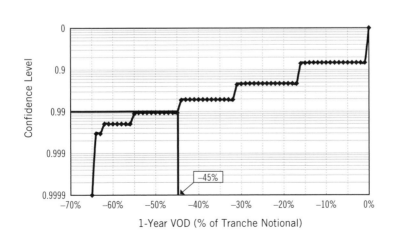

FIGURE **5.9** *One-Year VOD Cumulative Distribution of Selling Equity Tranche Protection (CDX.NA.IG.4, March 31, 2005)*

Market Risk

There are mainly two market risks in synthetic CDOs: credit-spread risk and correlation risk. Even though interest-rate risk still exists, it is far less important compared to spread and correlation risk.

Credit-Spread Risk

While defaults certainly have the largest impact on a credit derivatives position, they are relatively rare. As recent events (for example, GMAC in May 2005) illustrate, investors in credit derivatives are exposed to significant risks even if no defaults actually occur. While for single-name CDSs the nature of market risks is fairly intuitive, they are not always so for more complicated products, such as synthetic CDOs.

Similar to the single-name CDS, a simple measure of credit-spread sensitivity for the synthetic CDO is the marginal CS01 (that is, for a particular obligor, the mark-to-market change of the tranche if the credit spread is increased by 1 bp). For example, for the CDX.NA.IG.4 as of March 31, 2005, the marginal CS01 for GMAC is –0.007% of equity tranche notional. In other words, if GMAC's spreads curve shifts up 1bp, the equity tranche protection seller will lose –0.007% of tranche notional.

Marginal CS01 is an essential spread sensitivity measure, but it is not enough for synthetic CDO risk capture for two reasons: (1) marginal CS01 doesn't show the spread-gamma effects and (2) there are many names in the pool that may move together or may disperse (that is, some tightening and others widening). **FIGURE 5.10** shows the spread sensitivities for the seller of the equity tranche protection by perturbing different numbers of names in the pool and by using different magnitudes of spreads widening: For example, a 10 basis point spread widening in one name is compared to a 5 basis point spread widening in two names, and so on.

For small spread shocks, the tranche responds approximately linearly insofar as the impact of shocking multiple names simultaneously (by a small amount) is not too far from the sum of the individual marginal impacts. However, with larger spreads shocks, the nonlinear dependence of the tranche mark-to-market with respect to the credit spreads of the reference issuers manifests itself in different ways, depending on how much the spreads widen (or tighten) and how many names in the pool undergo spread widening (or tightening). These nonlinearities will come to fore when we discuss hedging CS01 exposures arising from CDO tranches with single-name CDS (Chapter 6). Even though Figure 5.10 presents a good picture of the spread sensitivities and gamma effects for the equity tranche protection seller, it doesn't show the scenarios that some name spreads widen while other spreads narrow (that is, spread dispersion).

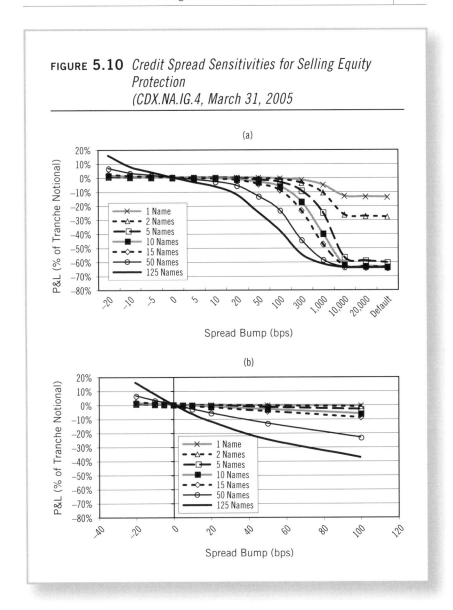

FIGURE **5.10** *Credit Spread Sensitivities for Selling Equity Protection (CDX.NA.IG.4, March 31, 2005*

Correlation Risk

One important difference between the single-name CDS and the synthetic CDO is the correlation variable. The correlation among the names in the underlying pool in the synthetic CDO can significantly impact the P&L of holding a position in a synthetic CDO. **FIGURE 5.11** demonstrates the correlation impact for the 0%–3% CDX.NA.IG.4 (March 31, 2005) equity tranche protection seller. As shown in Figure 5.11, for an equity protection seller, the investor is long correlation. In other words, the inves-

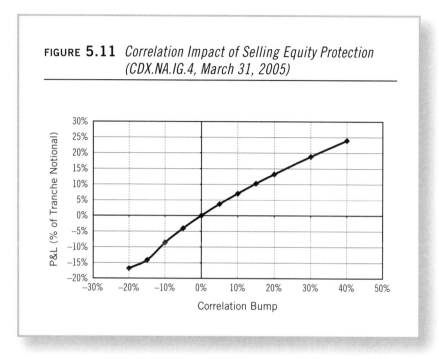

FIGURE **5.11** *Correlation Impact of Selling Equity Protection (CDX.NA.IG.4, March 31, 2005)*

tor will gain if the correlation of the underlying pool increases, and will lose if the correlation decreases.

The correlation effect will be reversed if an investor sells protection on the senior tranche. A senior tranche protection seller is short correlation. In other words, the senior tranche protection seller will lose if the correlation goes up.

If the pool has uncorrelated assets, then the chance of multiple obligors defaulting will be rare, relative to the case of high correlation, thereby helping the senior tranche protection seller. With low correlation, there is also less of a chance of multiple obligors surviving, thereby hurting the equity tranche.

In May 2005, the synthetic CDO market received a shock associated with the market realizing the vulnerability of popular synthetic CDO trading strategies (elaborated in Chapter 6) to idiosyncratic credit events—as manifested in the auto sector widening and downgrades. This realization and the initial mark-to-market losses led to hedge fund trades unwinding, which exacerbated the effect and led to the 10% drop in equity tranche implied correlation.

FIGURE 5.12 shows the credit spreads of the index CDX.NA.IG. (series 3 and 4), Ford Motor Credit, GMAC (which are constituents of CDX. NA.IG.), and the up-front payment of the equity tranche. **FIGURE 5.13** additionally highlights the relationship between the equity tranche im-

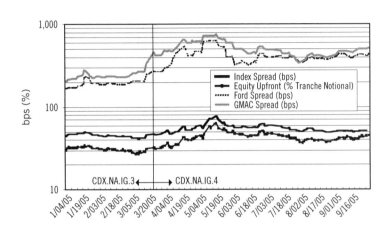

FIGURE **5.12** *Equity Up-front Payment, Credit Spreads of CDX.NA.IG (Series 3 and 4), Ford Motor Credit, and GMAC*

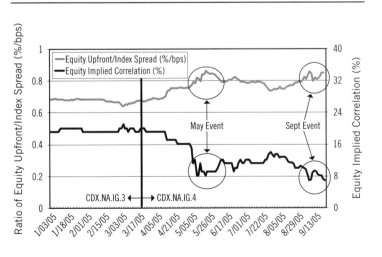

FIGURE **5.13** *Equity Implied Correlation Versus Ratio of Equity Up-front Payment over Index Spread for CDX.NA.IG (Series 3 and 4)*

plied correlation and the cost of purchasing equity protection relative to the cost of purchasing index protection. This relative measure of an equity tranche can be observed by simply dividing the up-front payment (needed to purchase equity protection) by the reference index spread (that is, percent up-front per unit index spread in bps). Figure 5.12 clearly shows that in May 2005 the widening of Ford and GMAC's credit spreads preceded the credit spread widening of the index. The May 2005 correlation "meltdown" (Figure 5.13) was "explainable" (in hindsight) as an increase in the market price of risk with respect to idiosyncratic spread widening. Figure 5.13 also depicts the ratio of the equity up-front payment over the index spread (that is, the percentage of equity tranche up-front payment for every bp of the index credit spread). The higher this ratio is, the greater the reimbursement to the equity tranche protection seller for taking on credit risk relative to a seller of protection on the index. Figure 5.13 shows that the equity tranche protection seller gets paid a larger up-front per unit index credit spread when the implied correlation drops. Thus, the implied correlation can be viewed as a mechanism for the market to express its risk tolerance above and beyond its beliefs in correlation among credits in the pool, in addition to demand and supply considerations in the market.

Chapter Notes

1. This ignores the counterparty credit risk between the protection buyer and protection seller.

2. For bibliographic references, please see page 177.

CHAPTER 6

Risk Management for Multistrategy Funds

CHRISTOPH KLEIN

As stated in Chapter 1, a multistrategy framework confers important advantages to a fund, among them the ability to exploit a wider range of market situations and integrate new credit instruments as they are developed. A multistrategy approach also presents risk management challenges.

This section will describe, in an abbreviated manner, a possible approach to meeting this challenge.

Structure

Within the credit subfund, the research, trading, and portfolio management functions are combined into a single *credit team*. This team approach provides a competitive advantage by aiding in the recognition of trading opportunities and the rapid structure and execution of trading strategies as well as permanent position monitoring and portfolio balancing.

Investment Restrictions

Very often internal limits at the single-name credit long positions and portfolio levels are established (see **FIGURE 6.1**). These restrictions enforce diversification and can reduce downside risk, especially the credit jump to default risk.

Economic leverage is calculated as the total economic exposure divided by the (sub-) fund's capital. Economic exposure is the sum of all long

FIGURE **6.1** *Single-Name Long Credit Exposure*

Fund Size	ECONOMIC LEVERAGE < 3		ECONOMIC LEVERAGE < 3 x < 5		ECONOMIC LEVERAGE > 5	
	100M	300M	100M	300M	100M	300M
Obligor BBB– or better	10%	8%	7.5%	6%	7%	5.5%
Obligor rating B	7%	5%	6%	5%	5%	4%
Obligor lower than B–	5%	4%	4%	3%	3%	2%

positions plus the sum of all PVs of all short positions. The reason for the asymmetric treatment of longs and shorts is that on a credit long position the entire notional or market value can be lost (assuming a zero recovery), whereas in a short position the maximum loss is limited to a spread tightening to zero. Netting of long and short positions is only allowed when the reference entity is exactly similar (as in issuer credit curve trades). The economic leverage of the fund is limited to ten times.

Furthermore, there are limits on credit instruments as, for example, investments in convertible bonds are limited to 15% of the economic exposure. Other investment restrictions include dimensions like maximum exposure to non-OECD countries or maximum net long sector exposures.

Risk Management

Next, we will recap and expand the information in the strategy section and explain the measurement and mitigation of the credit fund's different risk dimensions.

Currency Risk

The credit fund could seek to hedge all currency exposure using spot and forward foreign exchange transactions on a dynamic basis or borrow portions in the same currency.

Interest-Rate Risk

The credit fund could seek to hedge all interest-rate exposure. However, precise hedges may be difficult and costly to achieve so a limited range of interest-rate instruments may be used. As an example, within the corporate bond portfolio strategies (strategies 1 and 2) the maximum deviation in modified duration can amount to 0.3 years. Despite this issue, the fund controls and reduces any excessive interest-rate curve risks by using appropriate futures and options or trading the appropriate benchmark government bonds. To the extent that the credit instrument is in a currency other than U.S. dollars (the fund's base currency), the interest-rate risk will be hedged using interest-rate instruments in the same currency to reduce curve differential risk.

Credit Market Exposure

The credit fund's strategies generally seek to extract positive returns by constructing long-short pairs (for example, single names, portfolio versus index). As such, the general market exposure risk will be largely neutral, and outright directional market exposure risk will be relatively low as compared to a long-only fund. Hedging at the credit relative-value level will be done primarily via CDSs at the sector and index level. Hedging may be done on a spread duration and credit beta-adjusted basis. The concept of credit beta is crucial to credit-spread risk management and is often based on historical covariances (like equity betas) and the ratio of single-issuer spread versus the credit-market spread (like five-year iTraxx main) to capture latest price actions in an efficient way.

Besides the general credit-market exposure measured by the sum of every single position's credit beta multiplied by DV01, there are finer dimensions to consider. The basis exposure is the difference between corporate-bond and synthetic credit positions. In late 2006, the development of new credit structures like constant proportion debt obligations (CPDOs) led to an outperformance of CDS spreads versus corporate-bond spreads and to a change in the basis.

Credit curves can steepen, first in the dimension of maturities as ten-year credit spreads can widen more than five-year credit spreads; second, in the dimension of credit quality as spreads of BB-rated issuers might widen more than spreads of better-rated issuers. These credit risk exposures are considered for single-credit positions and certainly for the overall credit portfolio.

Equity Risk

A credit fund will occasionally hedge the equity component of a convertible position or capital structure trade. Choosing appropriate exposure ratios can mitigate the equity risk in debt-equity trades. On a portfolio level, the remaining equity-market exposure can be hedged with equity futures or equity put options.

Liquidity Risk

The vast majority (minimum 90%) of the instruments held by the fund must be liquid; defined as the bid-ask spread of less than 1% of the instrument's price. Price data and tradeable bids must be available at least on a daily basis.

Allocation of the Portfolio

The credit fund must decide how to allocate its investments among the various strategies explained in Chapter 1 in order to optimize risk-adjusted portfolio returns. This allocation must conform to the investment restrictions and will depend on prevailing and future expected market conditions.

Scenario 1 in **FIGURE 6.2** represents the market in 2001–2002. In this equity crash, the optimum allocation to convertibles would have been zero. Carry trades assuming stable spreads also would not have worked given the high spread volatilities. On the other hand, identifying credit short trades can be highly profitable due to the high number of defaults. This scenario contrasts with scenario 3, which we believe reflects the current market environment (early 2007).

The table in Figure 6.2 illustrates how a multistrategy approach greatly enhances flexibility when faced with changing market conditions. By aiding in the creation of a more diversified portfolio, the fund's ability to generate stable and attractive returns over time will be enhanced.

FIGURE **6.2** *Strategy Performance in Various Market Scenarios*

Scenarios	STRATEGY 1	STRATEGY 2	STRATEGY 3A
1. Spreads widen, shares fall, volatility increases, higher number of defaults	good	very good	poor
2. Spreads tighten, shares flat, volatility falling, few defaults	good	moderate	very good
3. Spreads stable, spread correlation decreases, shares rise, volatility flat or rising, few defaults	good	moderate	good

Strategy 1: Corporates Selection—Select Winners	Strategy 5: Credit Derivatives Trades
Strategy 2: Corporates Selection—Sell Underperformers	Strategy 6: Credit Correlation Trades
Strategy 3a: Credit Carry Trades	Strategy 7: Credit Structure Trades
Strategy 3b: Credit Directional Trades	Strategy 8: Capital Structure Trades
Strategy 4: Convertibles Selection	

Portfolio Monitoring Tools

Using a system that integrates trading, position valuation, and portfolio monitoring into a sophisticated, comprehensive risk management tool offers several advantages.

All trades should be recorded in the same system, which ensures compliance with regulatory and internal guidelines. This system is capable of revaluing the entire portfolio on an intraday basis, generating comprehensive mark-to-market valuations and risk assessments at the instrument, trade, strategy, sector, or portfolio levels. This intraday revaluation capacity can produce stress tests and perform scenario analyses (refer to **FIGURE 6.3**). With this tool, we can assess the key dimensions (interest rates, credit spreads, equity market movements and changes in equity volatility). By considering all positions (long and short) simultaneously, this approach enables the fund to detect any portfolio biases on an ongoing basis and to get a better understanding and feeling for this rather complex portfolio.

By integrating the fund's current portfolio with real-time and historical market information, the scenario analysis capacity of the system can be harnessed to evaluate the impact potential trades will have on the overall portfolio and suggest new trading opportunities.

Additionally, early warning indicator technology should be employed

STRATEGY 3B	STRATEGY 4	STRATEGY 5	STRATEGY 6	STRATEGY 7	STRATEGY 8
very good	poor	very good	good	poor	good
good	poor	poor	good	good	moderate
good	very good	moderate	moderate	good	good

FIGURE **6.3** *Risk Analysis and Stress Testing*

FACTORS OR BETAS	CREDIT BETA ADJUSTED NET DV01	IN % OF FUND'S CAPITAL
Interest-rate exposure	Interest-rate DV01 close to zero	Almost zero
Currency exposure	Almost zero	Almost zero
Market exposure (Net credit beta DV01)	22,209 *This means the fund is net credit market short as a 1 bp widening leads to a profit of 22,209.*	0.14%
Basis exposure (Corporate bonds versus CDS)	−21,946	−0.14%
Curve maturity exposure (Steepening/flat)	−32,489	−0.20%
Credit quality steepener (Xover-IG)	−19,959	−0.12%
Sector exposure (Fin/Corp)	−18,493	−0.11%
Equity market exposure	Currently zero *This measures the portfolio impact of a decrease of 1% in equity markets.*	Currently zero
Equity volatility exposure	Currently zero *This measures the portfolio impact of a decrease of 1% in equity market volatility.*	Currently zero

that scans credit and equity markets for an indication of any potential price movements or volatility changes. By alerting the fund's managers to potential problems in the credit markets before they fully materialize, the managers take steps to mitigate unwanted risk and seek to generate profitable trading opportunities.

This integrated platform would provide the fund manager with a competitive advantage and is an important factor in achieving the fund's objective of outperforming the market by focusing on alpha generation while strictly controlling and limiting all relevant factor exposures.

Summary

This chapter described a set of strategies for exploiting relative value opportunities within the credit markets and makes the case that a multistrategy approach will provide the flexibility to select the strategy and credit instruments best suited to the current situation within an ever-changing environment.

We described a practical approach to effectively implement such a strategy emphasizing the importance of thorough fundamental analysis, an integrated organizational structure, and the development of sophisticated risk-management technology.

CHAPTER 7

Integrating Event Risk in Portfolio Construction

ALLA GIL

T he market developments of 2001 and 2002, when five to six standard deviation events repeatedly occurred one after another, shocked many investors. They were surprised because they viewed the market through the lens of normal distribution, in which the probability of an event more than three standard deviations from the mean approaches zero. When considering short-term market risk exposure, a normal distribution is a reasonable approximation. But when considering credit risks, default events don't fit easily onto a bell curve. This is because there are more default events than normal distribution allows for. This situation is described by another kind of distribution curve called "leptokurtic" or "fat-tailed." (*Fat-tailed* refers to the distinctive shape of the part of the curve onto which extreme events fall.) In fat-tailed distribution, standard deviation does not represent a meaningful measure of risk. Risk managers have intuitively understood this fundamental distinction in risk distributions. Financial institutions used to have different approaches to market and credit risks that were handled by separate departments.

The processes underlying market and credit risk differ. This is why a different distribution curve describes each:

❏ *Market risk* is associated with two-sided (but not necessarily symmetric) exposure: market volatility, up and down movements and recoverable losses. For example, yield curves (exchange rates, equity prices, spreads, etc.) can go up or down and generate gains or losses for the portfolio.

❏ *Credit risk* is associated with one-sided exposure: the abrupt and irrecoverable loss of default or a credit-rating downgrade. A default is one-sided because, most of the time (except for distressed-market players) an investor must realize losses right away; he can't wait for the value to "come back." The same is sometimes true for a downgrade: an investment-grade portfolio manager cannot wait for the BB-rated name to get upgraded, no matter how much he believes in the quality of the issuer; he has to sell the name and realize his losses almost immediately after the issuer has fallen out of the investment-grade category.

The insurance industry has long understood how different types of risk follow different distribution patterns and has developed a method (extreme value theory) to cope with it. But this method does not apply directly to financial risks because it assumes that the tail of a distribution curve is independent from its central bell-shaped part. This is a valid assumption for insurance risk (earthquakes, floods, fires, and other catastrophic events). However, in financial risks, tails are not totally independent. For example, every increase in spread level leads to some rise in probability of fatal downgrade or default.

This means that market risk (mostly driven by volatility of major market factors) has an impact on the probability of arrival of "one-sided" events (credit or other fat-tailed risk). This dynamic is very important for generating a realistic risk distribution for the overall portfolio.

This chapter presents a new approach, fat-tailed value at risk (FT-VaR), to analyzing financial risks affecting both sides of the balance sheet and proposes a way to cope with these risks. FT-VaR accommodates the rare events characteristic of stressful markets: periods of multiple defaults and entire industry-sector downgrades and times when correlations between the major drivers of risk break from their usual patterns, and the market moves from "normal" to "tail" behavior. Incorporating such dynamic correlations into the risk analysis is a critical feature of this approach.

The chapter is structured the following way:

❑ Section 1 describes the proposed methodology and explains why it is preferable to the other risk measures used for portfolios that include asset classes with event risk.

❑ Section 2 outlines new approaches to

—modeling underlying risk factors and dynamic correlation between them,

—estimating the probability of extreme events implied from the paths, and

—incorporating event behavior through simulating irrecoverable losses (jumps) and their impact on the overall portfolio.

❑ Section 3 presents the methodology for

—understanding and analyzing the resulting empirical distribution of integrated risk and

—constructing the efficient frontier for portfolios that include "event" driven asset classes.

❑ Section 4 focuses on

—risk budgeting, that is, allocating risks back to asset classes and risk buckets,

—strategic decision making based on this analysis (like reallocating excess liquidity into additional yield), and

—identifying a realistic and consistent way to implement these decisions and transitioning portfolios toward efficient frontiers.

Section 1: Defining Measures of Risk

FT-VaR is a risk measure that can be consistently used across different asset classes including ones with discontinuous behavior. This makes it possible to both specify the optimization objective (that is, focusing on the tails of distributions) and construct an efficient frontier. FT-VaR expands the standard value-at-risk (normal distribution-based VaR, ND-VaR) methodology, which was traditionally used for assessment of market risk, to cover extreme risk, dynamic correlations, and fat-tailed distribution characteristic of multiasset-class portfolios.

VaR has certain features that make its direct application to multiasset-class portfolios unadvisable. It typically relies on historical data, which cannot predict events that never happened in the past. Almost every major crisis in financial markets was viewed by investors as a "change in paradigm." Standard VaR assumes normal distribution of the overall risk. However, standard deviation, which is an appropriate measure of risk for such a distribution, is not a meaningful measure when extreme events can be present. Confidence intervals calculated as a number of standard deviations will likely not cover fat-tailed risks. And finally, VaR has a short-term horizon of analysis, while risk should be properly analyzed over three to five years for banks and ten years and longer for insurance companies and pension funds. For a portfolio of reasonably high-quality holdings, the probability of defaults, or significant equity deterioration, over a short-term horizon is negligible. But over a long-term horizon, there is a possibility of quality erosion followed by credit migration that can accumulate and make the risk of big losses quite substantial. Though life insurance companies and pension funds naturally look at long-term strategies because of the duration of their liabilities, they often underestimate risk accumulation dynamics, especially in equity and credit portfolios.

A natural extension of the standard VaR approach is to use economic

TABLE **7.1** *Comparison of VaR and Economic Capital as Measures of Risk*

Strengths and Weaknesses	Shortcomings of VaR remedied	Advantages of VaR preserved
ND-VaR	Approximates the historical portfolio outcomes as having normalized distribution of risk, calculates standard deviation of portfolio changes, and applies 2 to 3 standard deviation moves for 10- to 90-day time horizon to come up with confidence intervals for the future portfolio outcomes	Describes the probability of feasible losses, or the probability of NAV crossing the given threshold, and summarizes in a single measure the worst-case loss faced by a company over a target horizon with a given confidence interval
FT-VaR	Estimates historical parameters of underlying risk factors, simulates their future behavior for 3- to 10-year horizon while overlaying stressful conditions and possible extreme losses, obtains the natural (often fat-tailed) distribution of portfolio values based on the simulated paths, and calculates the implied 99% to 99.97% confidence intervals, which are not based on the number of standard deviations	The same

capital as a comprehensive measure of risk. Economic capital is defined here as the amount of capital to be held against the unexpected losses up to a given confidence interval. (This definition is consistent with Basel II terminology.) Evaluation of economic capital is based on simulating future market uncertainties followed by estimating portfolio values on each path. It incorporates simulation of fat-tail events with the probabilities embedded in the observable market variables (equity and other asset prices, yield and credit spread curves, and so on) on each random path. Economic capital can be evaluated for arbitrary confidence intervals (from 99.5% in one year to 97.5% in five years are commonly used levels) and for a sufficiently long-term horizon.

The new risk measure, FT-VaR, avoids the weaknesses of the traditional VaR, while retaining its strengths (see **TABLE 7.1**).

Understanding the nature of fat-tail behavior in the underlying drivers of risk is the first step in constructing the outcome distribution of portfolio risks.

It is empirically known that most distributions of financial risk are fat-tailed.[1] Yet standard asset allocation and ALM methodologies approximate risks as being normally or lognormally distributed. This works quite well under stable covariance assumptions. The problem arises in crisis times, when volatilities and correlations of observable market variables are very high, causing much higher probability of extreme events. In such situations, approximating fat tails with normal or lognormal distributions makes it impossible to predict rare or unique events and analyze their impact on the overall performance, an essential task for any risk management process.

To illustrate the dynamic nature of distribution parameters, consider the correlation between a stock price and a spread of the same issuer. On a day-to-day basis it remains surprisingly low. This means that in the absence of any fundamental news about the company, the systemic correlation overwhelms the idiosyncratic one.

The recent crisis at General Motors Corporation is a relevant case study. The correlation of returns on the company's equity with the issuer credit spread changed dramatically in the spring of 2005 during financial crisis: it jumped from the long-term average of –46% to –90% (see **TABLE 7.2**).

TABLE 7.2 *Correlation of GM's Credit Spreads and Equity Returns Over Time*

PERIOD	DATES	CORRELATION (SPREAD VS. EQUITY)
Longer-term, precrisis	6/02–2/05	–46%
During crisis	2/05–4/05	–90%

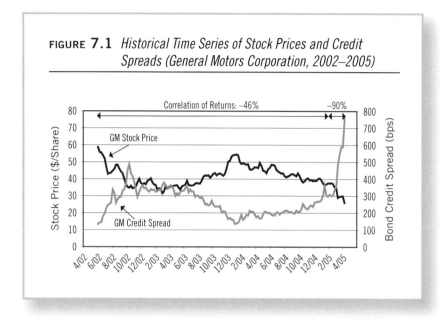

FIGURE **7.1** *Historical Time Series of Stock Prices and Credit Spreads (General Motors Corporation, 2002–2005)*

Stock prices follow the dynamics of the equity market, and corporate yields follow the spread market. If there is bad news about the company, the correlation suddenly becomes almost perfect, as the spread spikes and equity price tumbles (see **FIGURE 7.1**). When the issuer under stress is big enough, it can affect the entire industry sector or even an entire asset class.

The turmoil at AIG in 2005 demonstrates how the relatively stable, long-term correlation of the company's stock price with the equity market changes dramatically during crisis times. Similarly, the correlation of the company credit spreads and the industry sector spreads gets distorted (see **TABLE 7.3**).

Portfolio managers who focus on outperforming a given benchmark often ignore this dynamic. Sometimes investors who don't explicitly use credit instruments in their portfolios assume that their assets are immunized from fat-tailed risk, especially if their equity allocations follow a standard benchmark, such as one of equity indexes. But equity is just another form of exposure to an issuer. One of the most widely used approaches to pricing and managing credit risk is based on equity market information.[2] Unless a portfolio of equity holdings is highly diversified, it might also be exposed to a fat-tailed distribution of risk. An actual portfolio is always different from the benchmark it replicates, and hopefully outperforms, on a daily basis. If a major catastrophic event happens, the portfolio manager cannot just replace the "fallen angel" as would the benchmark. He has to deal with the long-term consequences of realized losses. To help portfolio

TABLE 7.3 *Correlations between the Company and the Market*

PERIOD	DATES	SPREAD CORRELATION: ISSUER VS. SECTOR SPREAD	EQUITY CORRELATION: COMPANY VS. S&P 500
Longer-term, 52-week precrisis	3/04–3/05	70%	50%
During crisis	3/05–4/05	–51%	10%

managers to avoid these hidden pockets of risk, we suggest using credit market information that can offer an additional insight to estimate embedded probabilities of downgrades and defaults. These probabilities are used to simulate unexpected absolute losses.

The equity market carries as much fundamental information about the credit quality of issuers as corporate debt. Equities just have more systemic risk so it is harder to "clean the noise" and extract the pure probabilities of default from stock prices. That's why the most efficient ways to measure credit risk are hybrid ones, combining information from equity and credit markets.

The bell-shaped part of the risk-distribution curve (where the losses are recoverable) describes the typical, volatile behavior of an equity investment. In crisis times this changes dramatically. Every corporate default impacts equity holdings, both the specific stock and the industry group. When defaults occur more frequently than usual they can generate a "domino effect," which has a more significant impact on respective sectors and the overall market.

Standard asset allocation methodologies failed to understand the financial crisis of the early 2000s. In large part this is because they did not incorporate the probability of fat-tail events into their analyses.

However, if the tails of risk distributions are modeled taking into account losses due to rare events and dynamic correlations between different asset classes, an investor can comprehend the "domino effect." Losses that seemed to be "impossible" can happen with greater than 5% probability (a standard confidence interval for VaR analysis).

What follows will demonstrate the difference between a traditional risk analysis, based on joint lognormal distributions with static covariance, and the proposed event analysis approach that considers the full dynamic impact of substantial downgrades and defaults in an industry

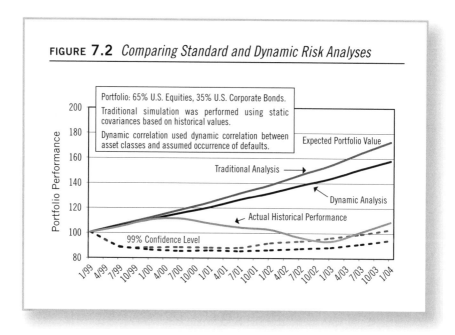

FIGURE **7.2** *Comparing Standard and Dynamic Risk Analyses*

sector. Consider a typical pension fund portfolio: 65% of equity and 35% fixed income.

FIGURE 7.2 shows the actual historic behavior of such a portfolio between 1999 and 2003; the expected and the 99% worst-case outcome predicted by a standard risk assessment; and the same confidence interval generated by considering adverse credit events and their combined impact on these two asset classes. Both traditional and dynamic analyses were performed based on the information available in 1999.

As the graphs show, the lowest value that this static portfolio exhibited historically was not predicted by traditional risk measures. But if the risk distribution were constructed in January of 1999 incorporating the possibility of extreme events, there would be a more realistic picture of the future outcomes.

Section 2: Bottom-Up Methodology

We identified two major categories of risk: two-sided or reversible exposures (representing regular market volatilities), and one-sided exposures associated with irreversible losses due to extreme events (for example, defaults or necessity to sell some assets in order to cut losses). The former represents the central, bell-shaped part of risk distribution. It is handled very well by traditional risk management methodologies. The latter reflects the tail of the distribution. It is driven by unusually high probabilities of extreme events and increased correlations among them. These two types of risk are not independent: the regular uncertainties in "normal" market environments imply some probability of "extreme" markets with tail events. Methodologies that calibrate the tails of the distribution separately from the central part (for example, extreme value theory) underestimate the increased frequency of extreme events when volatilities and correlations spike.

We propose an approach that consistently considers both types of risk while dynamically assessing their interdependent relationship. To do so we use a bottom-up method for aggregating risk.

We start with modeling observable drivers of risk for the major asset classes in the portfolio, such as yield and credit curves, equity and real estate values, and currency and commodity prices. One can obtain historical time series for these variables and estimate their joint distribution parameters. Most of these risk factors (for example, yields, spreads) are modeled traditionally as lognormally (or normally) distributed compatible with well-accepted pricing techniques for specific market instruments.

We use Monte Carlo simulation to obtain the future values of these observable risk factors. The simulation parameters (for example, trends, volatilities, and correlations) can be estimated based on historical time series or can be imposed by specific economic views or desired stress-testing scenarios. On each path we evaluate the probability of extreme events and simulate them as well. For example, each sample of a credit spread implies a certain probability of default;[3] this probability is used to simulate default events on this path; if default happened, the value of the investment declines to the recovery level.

As was noticed previously, another important source of fat-tailed distribution, besides extreme events, is the dynamic behavior of correlations. It is well known that every time the market undergoes a major crisis, correlations can spike substantially or even change sign.

Yet estimating these dynamic correlations is a very complicated process. In order to approximate the real-market environment and have a transparent and intuitive risk assessment framework, we model two different types of dynamic correlations.

The first one reflects the effects of the changes in macroeconomic regimes. As economic conditions change, we can observe high, low, and average yield curve levels; various credit cycles; equity markets out- or underperforming other classes; and so on. These changes are usually observed over long enough periods so that the specific correlations can be evaluated. There are certain levels of the underlying market variables representative for these periods. For example, in U.S. markets, the average "band" for the 10-year Treasury rate has been between 4% and 6%. The long-term average was 5.3%. Outside of these bounds we classify the rates as being respectively high or low. Normal market conditions generally mean that equity market (high risk/high return) outperforms the other asset classes. Within a relatively tight range around the mean, equity and interest-rate dynamics are likely to have fairly weak negative correlation (–10% in our example). Outside that range, higher than usual rates have stronger negative correlation with equities (–50%); in the low yield curve environment, the long-term rates are positively correlated with equity returns, as we observed in the markets in the past few years (see **TABLE 7.4**). By changing correlations between the simulated variables according to this pattern, it is possible to replicate historically observed behavior.

The second type of dynamic correlation is event driven. The correlations are defined implicitly on the simulated paths. Every time a major event happens, it might impact multiple asset classes. One of the major difficulties of understanding risks on a portfolio level is in capturing the synchronous behavior of exposures across different asset classes. A typical situation, for example, is when a seemingly very safe name is present in fixed income and equity portfolios simultaneously. On top of that, the same name is in collateral pools of every CDO tranche in the portfolio. The exposure to this name in each asset class might be within the limit. But in case of an unexpected event (for example, default), it might turn out that the overall portfolio exposure to this name was well over the limit!

The same can happen for the industry concentration: if some rare events happen to multiple names in an industry, it can simultaneously impact all asset classes exposed to this industry.

To estimate this type of correlation, we jointly simulate equity price and credit spreads. On a path where an issuer defaults, we force the respective stock to lose 90% to 95% of the value. We also adjust holdings in the same industry across all asset classes in accordance with their

TABLE 7.4 *Correlation Between Fixed Income and Equity Markets*

RATE ENVIRONMENT	CORRELATION OF EQUITY RETURNS AND LONG-TERM RATES
High (6+%)	–50%
Average (4.3%–6%)	–10%
Low (below 4.3)	40%

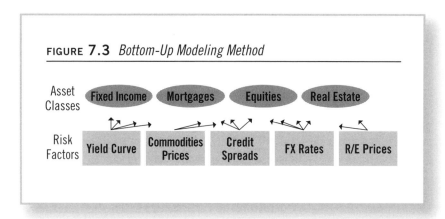

FIGURE **7.3** *Bottom-Up Modeling Method*

historical reaction to defaults and other events producing abrupt big losses. Because of the relatively high correlation between the names in the industry, substantial downturn of several names will adversely impact the entire industry.

Alternative investments, particularly fund of funds (FoF), might appear to be very attractive, but they should be approached carefully, only after establishing that they can diversify existing portfolio holdings and fit the required risk profile. We have estimated that on average FoF might have 1.6% to 1.7% annual probability of a jump (significant loss of value) and applied this to generated paths for these asset class holdings.

After simulating all these underlying risk factors with overlaid rare events, we run the entire portfolio through the generated paths. This way we capture the correlations between the asset classes in the portfolio in a natural way: a change in correlations is driven by event impact on respective underlying risk factors (see **FIGURE 7.3**).

The resulting empirical distribution of the overall portfolio values demonstrates fat tails because of extreme events and dynamic correlations. Now it is possible to calculate expected value and any required confidence intervals for portfolio performance and obtain the economic capital (fat-tailed VaR) measure for the portfolio.

Is the Current Portfolio Optimal?

After estimating the overall risk distribution for the portfolio and calculating the amount of economic capital necessary to cover unexpected losses (defined as a difference between the expected portfolio value and its worst-case outcome with a prespecified confidence interval), we can identify whether it is possible to improve the risk-return relationship. In order to do this, we need to construct an efficient frontier: a collection of optimal portfolios that for each level of risk has maximum expected return. If the current portfolio is not on the frontier, it is possible to either improve portfolio returns for the same capital requirements or reduce capital needs without increasing the risk. In either case, capital efficiency increases.

The key feature distinguishing such efficient frontier (constructed with economic capital as a measure of risk) is explicit consideration of rare events and their impact on the tails of risk distribution.[4] The introduction of new asset classes modifies the frontier. The portfolio manager can observe the strategic effect of adding new asset classes to his portfolio (for example, whether this helps to position the portfolio closer to the desired part of the frontier).

To construct the efficient frontier, modify the weights of asset classes within the portfolio and find the combination of weights that would produce the highest expected return for the given amount of economic capital. To calculate the values of the objective function and constraints, we use the same simulation paths as for the underlying drivers of portfolio uncertainty. Then we evaluate the portfolio (with the new set of weights for the asset classes) on these paths and obtain the full distribution of risk for each "trial" set of weights. We use nonlinear optimization to find the combination of weights that gives the best portfolio return subject to given economic capital constraint. The most appropriate optimization

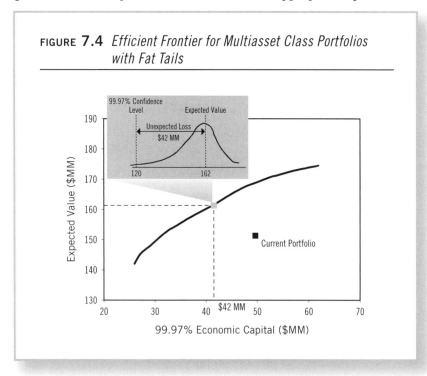

FIGURE **7.4** *Efficient Frontier for Multiasset Class Portfolios with Fat Tails*

algorithm for this problem is one that doesn't require the closed-form calculation of gradient or second order derivatives (quasi-Newton methods or any type of heuristic approaches: genetic algorithms or simulating annealing[5]).

Transitioning to the efficient frontier requires either buying or selling asset classes or modifying the portfolio's risk profile by overlaying derivatives instruments. When deciding on strategic asset allocations, it is very important to understand the marginal impact of a new asset class on the efficient frontier.

If the initial portfolio didn't contain structured credit instruments, for example, one could assume that adding this new asset class would increase both risk and return of the existing portfolio.

In reality, a new asset class might introduce an additional degree of freedom to increase returns without increasing risks; the entire frontier moves up.

The standard analysis of new asset classes on a stand-alone basis, without understanding the fat tails of the distributions, might miss some hidden pockets of risk. These risks in either the original portfolio or the proposed addition might be fully acceptable. But in combination, they can change the concentrations and correlation dynamics of the overall portfolio. Marginal contribution of risk can be different for the same asset added to different portfolios. The only way to determine the marginal economic capital of a new addition is to subtract the capital needs of an original portfolio from the expanded one. The ideal addition is the one that doesn't increase capital needs. The suggested approach to constructing an efficient portfolio with economic capital as a measure of risk allows us to incorporate all these interrelations and avoid the pitfalls of a stand-alone analysis.

The following example illustrates the previous points by constructing the efficient frontiers for fixed income portfolios with and without structured credit as a potential asset class (see **FIGURE 7.5** on page 136).

In this example, we first constructed the frontier for the different combination of sovereign (rated AAA and AA) and corporate bonds (rated A and A–). Then we analyzed the impact of adding a sample structured credit product.

We generated the paths for all the instruments in the current portfolio and the entire collateral pool of a considered CDO tranche according to the simulation methodology described previously. We calculate losses on each path the following way: if the loss came from the original portfolio, it is included as a full loss after recovery; if the loss came from the collateral pool, it is recognized only if the previous losses on the same path have exhausted the subordination and the lower bound of the tranche reached.

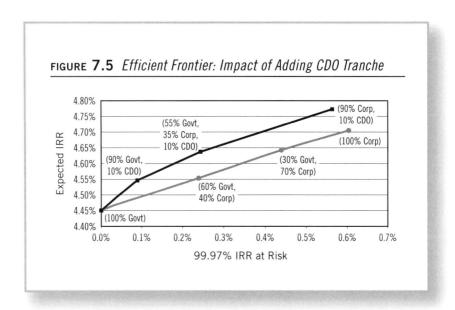

FIGURE **7.5** *Efficient Frontier: Impact of Adding CDO Tranche*

Once the tranche is "eaten through" (the upper bound of losses has been exceeded), there are no more losses on that path coming from the CDO addition.

Then we obtain the distributions of the internal rate of return (IRR) calculated on each path. The risk is measured as a difference between the expected value and the 99.97% worst-case outcome of IRR (as in economic capital calculation). We construct the efficient frontier for the original portfolio by selecting the weights between government and corporate holdings to optimize the distribution of IRR (ignoring the losses that came from the CDO tranche). Then we look at the joint losses and construct the frontier for the portfolio in which up to 10% of assets can be replaced with a CDO tranche of a reasonable rating (comparable with the corporate ratings in the original portfolio) with a collateral pool that optimally diversifies current holdings.

The graph in Figure 7.5 demonstrates that when we replace 10% of a portfolio with government holdings with a structured credit instrument (while keeping duration the same), it increases the overall portfolio risk expressed as 99.97% IRR at risk. At the same time, for a 100% corporate holdings portfolio, it is possible to reduce the overall risk by adding a CDO tranche from uncorrelated collateral pool. Added to a mixed portfolio (60% government, 40% corporate bonds), this tranche would produce a higher return for the same level of risk, thus, shifting upward the entire frontier. Adding a CDO tranche permits asset managers to achieve improved portfolio efficiency.

Risk Budgeting or Top-Down Methodology

The next step after building the efficient frontier is deciding which position on the efficient frontier should serve as a target for the current portfolio and how to transition there. The first issue is a function of strategic considerations: does a financial institution have risk capacity, what is its business model, would it like to improve its return for the same level of risk or reduce risk without compromising yield. It is also possible that the regulatory regime requires a certain amount of capital that exceeds the current economic capital need. This might happen because Basel II doesn't give banks full credit for diversification of exposures. In this case, the institution might decide to increase its economic capital constraint to the level of regulatory capital and raise the expected returns respectively: if one is charged for the risk taking, one should enjoy the rewards associated with it.

The second issue, how to migrate portfolios toward the efficient frontier, requires rebalancing the capital among the different business lines. Target optimal portfolios might require increasing or reducing specific asset holdings that can be part of asset portfolios of different businesses within the organization. Rebalancing of these holdings should be done in such a way that individual businesses remain solvent and profitable. Thus, the senior management needs to know how much capital each business requires.

In the previous section, we were focusing on integrating the risks and understanding capital needs for the entire portfolio given the dynamic correlations between the asset classes and underlying risk factors. Now we must do the opposite: decompose the overall risk and allocate capital back to the different asset classes and risk categories. This will help an asset manager to choose the best way to improve capital distribution and position a portfolio on the frontier.

In order to allocate capital to different business lines or asset classes, we need to determine for each simulated path from where the losses came. In our approach this is directly traceable. Thus, we can calculate the distribution of risks specifically attributed to the asset class under consideration and identify the amount of capital necessary to cover the unexpected losses for this asset class.

Because of some risk diversification, the economic capital requirements for the overall portfolio are usually less than the sum of capital needs of each asset class (**FIGURE 7.6**).

The same method of risk budgeting and reallocation can be done for specific types of risk. Usually long-term investors like insurance companies and pension funds have excess liquidity in their portfolios that can be traded for additional yield. Structured credit products represent a very

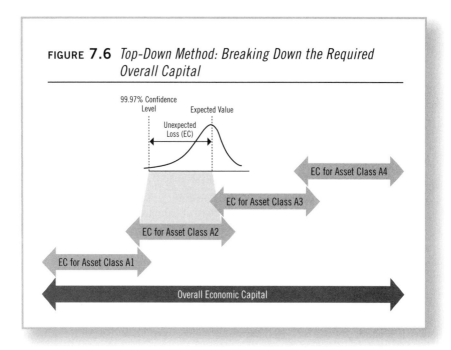

FIGURE 7.6 *Top-Down Method: Breaking Down the Required Overall Capital*

effective suite of instruments to implement this strategy. These products are relatively illiquid. But investors are usually well compensated through additional spreads. However, it is important to understand whether these spreads charged for illiquidity are enough to compensate investors for the rare and extreme events. We analyze this through substantial stress testing: simulating the same portfolios and their potential modifications using the parameters characteristic to historically stressful markets.

Like any other model, ours depends on the input parameters. It is a Monte Carlo simulation where the building blocks (trends and covariances for diffusive paths as well as probabilities and sizes of jumps) are estimated based on history or overlaid by an expert opinion. Since history is not a good predictor of the future and experts often are wrong, it is very important to know the sensitivity of the model to the input parameters. For strategic considerations, the main objective of the analysis is not to predict the future but to find a robust optimal portfolio modification that would be a valuable improvement over the current portfolio under broad market scenarios. To stress test the model, we calibrate the simulation parameters to the periods in history that were especially strenuous for this particular risk category (that is, default and credit migration probability matrices of year 2001 instead of historical average). Then we regenerate the simulation paths and reconstruct the frontier. Simultaneously the current portfolio position will respond to the changes in the simulated market environment.

If the planned modification is directionally still beneficial for the portfolio and positions it closer to the selected part of the frontier, it has passed the stress test.

Let's consider the previous example (Figure 7.5). We have assumed that both the current portfolio and the underlying collateral pool are static. Distressed market environment simultaneously impacts the existing portfolio and the new investment. Stress testing allows us to verify that such investments provide robust improvement to the portfolio performance.

In this example, the simulated distribution of portfolio values over time is quite sensitive to the fluctuations of rating transition rates.

We use Moody's historical average rating transition matrixes as a base case.[6] From Figure 7.5, we observe that by replacing up to 10% of the portfolio of 60% government and 40% corporate holdings with a CDO tranche, we improve the expected IRR by 9 bps for the same amount of required capital.

As a stress test we take one of the worst years in the U.S. recent (last twenty years) default history, 2001, and assume that such frequency of defaults will prevail for the next five years. This period was characterized by an almost tenfold increase in the probability of defaults, especially for A- and BBB-rated names.

By analyzing portfolios with and without the CDO tranche on the paths generated under these extreme assumptions, we can see that both have made parallel shifts: expected value went down by 10 bps and unexpected losses almost doubled. But on a relative basis, adding structured product still provided an improvement over the current portfolio. This means that, assuming total lack of liquidity in the market under this stressful scenario and inability to sell any of the holdings, the "illiquidity" cushion in the spread of CDO tranche and its diversification property pays off.

Summary

We have presented a framework based on economic capital considerations that is complementary to asset-liability and risk management methods used by most financial institutions. It naturally generates fat-tailed risk distributions based on implied dynamic correlations between different asset classes. It combines market (interest rate, foreign exchange, and equity index) and credit risk (corporate fixed income and lumpy equity) exposures on a consistent modeling platform.

The described approach allows us to estimate fat tails in the risk distributions of equity holdings consistently with credit exposures and identify the possible undesirable synchronous lumpiness in the overall portfolio. Even though we cannot predict which name will default, we can definitely assess the possible exposures to any name in case of its rapid deterioration.

We first have identified the firm's current economic capital profile. Then, we found the best way to reach an efficient frontier based on economic capital measure while controlling for regulatory issues. In particular, we identified structural overlay to maximize the return of the asset allocation strategy while holding unexpected losses at the level specified by risk policy guidelines.

This approach allows senior management to set up liability benchmarking, establish limits for risk budgeting, and monitor their economic capital demands.

Suggested methodology can be used for making strategic decisions on asset allocation.

And finally, it is possible to design optimal hedging strategies (taking into consideration regulatory constraints and risk policy guidelines) and immediately observe their impact on risk distribution.

Chapter Notes

1. Mandelbrot, 1963.

2. Kealhoffer, 1995; Kolyuoglu, 1998; and Merton, 1974.

3. Gil and Polyakov, Integration of Market and Credit Risk, 2003.

4. The classical notion of efficient frontier was based on historical data and portfolio variance as risk measure (Markowitz).

5. Gil and Polyakov, 2003.

6. Moody's, 2001.

References

E. Altman, A. Resti, and A. Sironi. 2001. Analyzing and explaining default recovery rates, Working Paper (Report submitted to ISDA).

Basel Committee on Banking Supervision. 1999. *A New Capital Adequacy Framework*. Basel, Switzerland: The Bank for International Settlements.

Basel Committee on Banking Supervision. 1999. *Credit Risk Modelling: Current Practices and Applications*. Basel, Switzerland: The Bank for International Settlements.

Basel Committee on Banking Supervision. 1988. *Internal Convergence of Capital Measurements and Capital Standards*. Basel, Switzerland: The Bank for International Settlements.

Fischer Black and Myron Scholes. 1973. The pricing of options and corporate liabilities. *Journal of Political Economy*, 81:637–54.

Christian Bluhm, Ludger Overbeck, Christoph Wagner. 2003. *An Introduction to Credit Risk Modeling*. Boca Raton, FL: Chapman & Hall/CRC.

Sanjiv Ranjan Das and Peter Tufano. (December 1994). Pricing credit-sensitive debt when interest rates, credit ratings and credit spreads are stochastic. Working paper, Harvard Business School.

Satyajit Das, editor. 1998. *Credit Derivatives: Trading and Management of Credit and Default Risk*. Wiley Frontiers in Finance. New York: John Wiley & Sons.

Bjorn Flesaker, Lane Houghston, Laurence Schreiber, and Lloyd Sprung. 1994. Taking all the credit. *Risk Magazine* 7:105–108.

Francis, Jack C., Joyce A. Frost, and J. Gregg Whittaker. 1999. *The Handbook of Credit Derivatives*. New York: McGraw-Hill.

A. Gil and T. Klymchuk. 2002. *Derivatives Use, Trading & Regulation*, Volume Seven, Number Four 2002, 324–336.

A. Gil and Y. Polyakov. 2003. "Integrating Market and Credit Risk in Fixed Income Portfolios" in Advances in portfolio construction and implementation, ed. S. Satchell & A. Scowcroft Burlington, MA: Butterworth-Heinemann Finance.

John Hull and Alan White. 2000. Valuing credit default swaps II: Modeling default correlations. Working paper, April.

Robert A. Jarrow, David Lando, and Stuart M. Turnbull. 1997. A Markov model for the term structure of credit risk spreads. *Review of Financial Studies* 10(2):481–523.

Stephen Kealhoffer. 1995. "Managing Default Risk in Derivative Portfolios" in *Derivative credit risk: Advances in measurement and management*. London: Renaissance Risk Publications.

H. Ugur Kolyuoglu and A. Hickman. October 1998. Reconcilable differences. *Risk Magazine*.

B. Mandelbrot. 1963. The variation of certain speculative prices. *Journal of Business* 36:394–419.

Robert C. Merton. 1974. On the pricing of corporate debt: The risk structure of interest rates. *Journal of Finance* 29:449–470.

Moody's. February 2001. Default and recovery rates of corporate bond issuers: 2000. D. Hamilton, G. Gupta, and A. Berhault.

T. Wilson. September/October 1997. Portfolio credit risk. *Risk*, 56–61, 111–117.

Chunsheng Zhou. 1997. A jump-diffusion approach to modeling credit risk and valuing defaultable securities. Finance and Economics Discussion Paper Series 1997/15, Board of Governors of the Federal Reserve System, March.

Chunsheng Zhou. 1997. Default Correlation: an analytical result. Finance and Economics Discussion Paper Series 1997/15, Board of Governors of the Federal Reserve System, May 1.

PART THREE

Pricing, Products, and Procedures

CHAPTER 8

Pricing Models

ROHAN DOUGLAS AND PETER RIVERA

Introduction

Valuation of credit derivatives has been one of the most exciting and challenging areas of financial engineering over the past few years. Pricing and hedging of these products pose unique challenges, and both the academic and professional communities have made considerable efforts to steadily improve the tools available. This effort has resulted in a constant and continuing stream of new approaches and ideas, particularly for some of the more recent basket products.

The wide variety of valuation approaches available reflects the diverse use of credit derivatives. Each of these approaches has different strengths and weaknesses, and the right choice depends on the intended use. Different uses for a valuation model include:

- ❑ Mark-to-market
- ❑ Hedge calculations
- ❑ Relative value analysis
- ❑ Capital reserve calculations
- ❑ Economic capital measurement
- ❑ Concentration/risk limits
- ❑ Portfolio optimization

To highlight the importance of using an appropriate valuation model, consider the task of calculating the mark-to-market of a trade. Here, typically, the objective is to calculate the value that the trade can be unwound. Unwind levels may be obtained from market participants. However, the best available approach may be to imply valuations from similar but more liquid securities. By construction, this type of model would be of no use for other applications such as relative value analysis.

This chapter gives a broad overview of the types of credit modeling available, which can serve as a road map for those trying to select the appropriate approach to any given situation.

Every credit derivative pricing approach contains two key components: the modeling of recovery (or the amount lost given a default) and the modeling of the default probability (the likelihood of experiencing a default).

Modeling Recovery

Recovery is the amount of an asset's value realized after default. This may be expressed in terms of

❑ A percentage of face
❑ The present value of the percentage of face
❑ A percentage of market value before default
❑ The present value of the percentage of market value

The current market standard is to quote recovery as a percentage of face. This, technically, is the closest match to the definition of recovery from the U.S. bankruptcy code, where a lender is owed the face amount plus the amount accrued on a defaulted bond. Even in the U.S. courts, the process can vary, however, and there is no definitive answer in this regard.

Although default is a relatively rare event, studies have been conducted, which serve as a starting point to understanding recovery rates (S&P and Moody's are the most commonly cited).

FIGURE 8.1 is a study by Moody's showing mean recovery rates on defaulted securities from 1982 to 2005. The recoveries are measured both in terms of the number of issues as well as market value. The value-weighed measure was introduced by Moody's to quantify events such as those that occurred in 2001 when there were a small number of very large defaults. The figure shows how realized recovery rates can vary significantly over time as well as across the capital structure.

FIGURE 8.2 shows the average recovery by industry type from an earlier Moody's survey. Again, the highlight from this figure is how much the recovery rate varies across industry as well as over time. In 2003, the average recovery varied from 5.3% for electric utilities to 76.8% for ocean transport.

FIGURE 8.3 shows the average recovery for senior unsecured bonds over time. This graph shows clearly how the recovery rate varies over time. There also is an interesting apparent cyclic nature to the variation of this rate over time.

FIGURE **8.1** *Average Recovery Rates for Corporate Debt Obligations, 1982–2005*

	ISSUER-WEIGHTED			VALUE-WEIGHTED		
	2005	2004	1982–2005	2005	2004	1982–2005
Bank Loans						
Sr. Secured	81.6	86.1	70	91.6	84.7	64.2
Sr. Unsecured	—	—	57.6	—	—	46.8
Bonds						
Equipment Trust	NA	28.3	59.3	NA	28.3	56.6
Sr. Secured	77.9	78.7	51.9	76.9	85.7	52.6
Sr. Unsecured	55.2	53.2	36	54.4	67.8	34.6
Sr. Subordinated	33.6	47.5	32.4	37	43.8	29.2
Subordinated	95.0*	82.9†	31.8	95.0*	78.4†	29.1
Jr. Subordinated	—	—	23.9	—	—	16.8
All Bonds	55.9	59.9	35.9	54.3	70.7	33.9
Preferred Stock	13.8	50.3	11.3	7.2	48.1	7.3
All Debt Instruments	54.5	63.3	37.7	53.5	69	35.8

* Based on one observation
† Based on three observations

Source: *Default and Recovery Rates of Corporate Bond Issuers*, Moody's, January 2006.

FIGURE 8.4 is a graph of the average recovery rate for each year versus the average default rate. It shows a strong correlation between the realized recovery rate and the average default rate, which reflects the overall economic condition. There are several possible explanations for this relationship. First, in difficult economic conditions, there are fewer buyers of the assets of a defaulted company, which leads to lower recovery rates. Second, a higher percentage of defaults during good economic times are surprise defaults for technical or other reasons, which leave more of the company's assets intact.

The correlation between recovery and average default rates is also reflected in a matching correlation between recovery and credit spreads.

FIGURE **8.2** *Average Recovery Rates by Industry Category*

INDUSTRY	2003	2002	1982–2003
Utility—Gas	48.0	54.6	51.5
Oil and Oil Services	NA	44.1	44.5
Hospitality	64.5	60.0	42.5
Utility—Electric	5.3	39.8	41.4
Transport—Ocean	76.8	31.0	38.8
Media, Broadcasting, and Cable	57.5	39.5	38.2
Transport—Surface	NA	37.9	36.6
Finance and Banking	18.8	25.6	36.3
Industrial	33.4	34.3	35.4
Retail	57.9	58.2	34.4
Transport—Air	22.6	24.9	34.3
Automotive	39.0	39.5	33.4
Health Care	52.2	47.0	32.7
Consumer Goods	54.0	22.8	32.5
Construction	22.5	23.0	31.9
Technology	9.4	36.7	29.5
Real Estate	NA	5.0	28.8
Steel	31.8	28.5	27.4
Telecommunications	45.9	21.4	23.2
Miscellaneous	69.5	46.5	39.5

Source: *Default and Recovery Rates of Corporate Bond Issuers, Moody's, January 2004.*

FIGURE 8.5 is an interesting frequency graph showing the number of occurrences for particular postdefault prices of senior unsecured debt. This graph depicts the distribution of recovery rates, which is strongly skewed towards lower recovery rates and is a reminder that average statistics are misleading when applied to the recovery rate. Recent common practice is to model the distribution of recovery rates

Source: *Default and Recovery Rates of Corporate Bond Issuers, Moody's, January 2005.*

FIGURE **8.3** *Average Annual Senior Unsecured Bond Recovery Rates, 1982–2005*

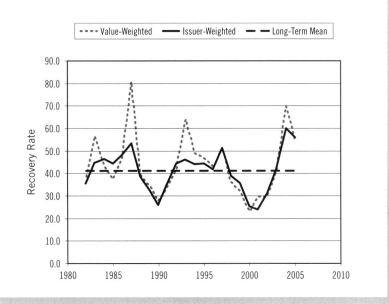

Source: *Default and Recovery Rates of Corporate Bond Issuers, Moody's, January 2006.*

FIGURE **8.4** *Correlation Between Defaults and Recoveries, 1983–2005*

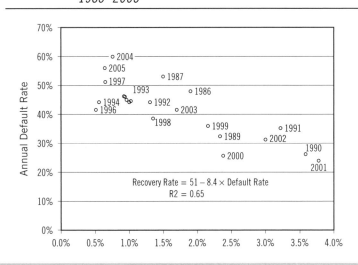

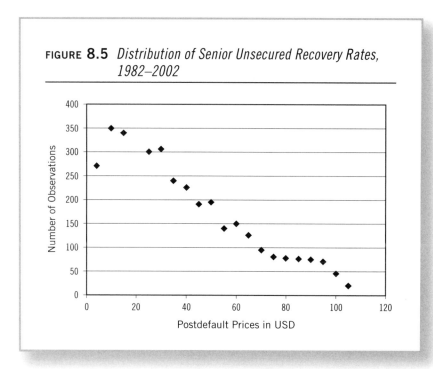

FIGURE **8.5** *Distribution of Senior Unsecured Recovery Rates, 1982–2002*

Source: Moody's Default and Recovery Report, 2003.

using a beta distribution parameterized to match the above distribution.

In conclusion, recovery rates vary significantly across industry, capital structure, and time. The distribution of recovery rates is highly skewed. Recovery rates are strongly cyclic and correlated with default rates, spreads, and overall economic activity.

The industry standard practice is to use one fixed recovery rate (typically 40%) for all credits. This works well in cases where models are first calibrated and then used for pricing using the same recovery assumptions, and recovery rate risk is being "passed through." In cases where recovery rate exposure is carried, care should be taken to model more accurately the nature of recovery rates.

Modeling Default

Modeling default involves calculating the likelihood that a particular company or reference credit will default. To model default as realistically as possible, intuitively one expects the likelihood of default to depend on credit fundamentals, such as:

❏ Industry
❏ Size
❏ Profitability
❏ Leverage

Source: *Default and Recovery Rates of Corporate Bond Issuers*, Moody's, January 2006.

FIGURE **8.6** *Global Corporate Bond Defaults*

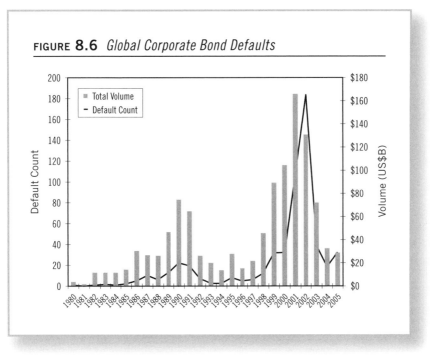

❑ Interest rates
❑ Market volatility
❑ Credit cycle

There are also other observable indicators from the market, such as:
❑ Observed defaults
❑ CDS quotes
❑ Bond prices

In addition, other derived data may be incorporated into modeling default, such as:
❑ Ratings
❑ Moody's KMV expected default frequencies (EDFs)

FIGURE 8.6 shows the average default rate for global corporate bonds between 1980 and 2005. It is striking how cyclic the average default rate appears to be and how closely related to overall economic conditions.

FIGURE 8.7 shows the average default rate for investment and speculative global corporate bonds between 1920 and 2005. This graph gives an even clearer perspective on the cyclical nature of default rates over time.

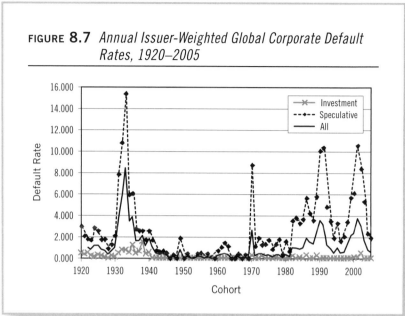

FIGURE **8.7** *Annual Issuer-Weighted Global Corporate Default Rates, 1920–2005*

Source: *Default and Recovery Rates of Corporate Bond Issuers,* Moody's, January 2006.

While there are many different ways to model the likelihood of default, in practice four types are most widely used.

1 Historical models that use historical data and rating agency data

FIGURE **8.8** *Average One-Year Whole Letter Rating Transition Rates, 1983–2005*

RATING FROM	RATING TO		
	AAA	AA	A
Aaa	94.65	5.21	0.00
Aa	4.43	92.28	1.38
A	0.00	2.90	91.73
Baa	0.00	0.00	8.88
Ba	0.00	0.00	0.00
B	0.00	0.00	0.00
Caa–C	0.00	0.00	0.00

2 Statistical models that use financial ratios and historical default data (for example, credit scoring)
3 Structural models that model the firm's assets and liabilities (for example, Merton and KMV)
4 Reduced-form models that imply risk-neutral default probabilities from market prices (for example, spread and hazard-rate models)

Hazard-rate models are currently the market standard for pricing, hedging, and risk analysis.

Historical Models

Historical models use historical default probabilities typically based on ratings agency data, such as bond migration studies.

FIGURE 8.8 shows the historical average transition rates for corporate bond issuers from 1983 to 2005. Each cell shows the average percentage of names that started the year with the rating on the left and ended the year with the rating in the column header. The Default column gives the average percentage of names of each rating that defaulted.

Historical models can be based on ratings agency data or on more granular internal ratings. Ratings are a well-known training indicator and are a relatively coarse way of estimating the likelihood of default. In general, using ratings-derived probabilities of default is more reasonable for large groups of companies and less reasonable for individual companies.

BAA	BA	B	CAA–C	DEFAULT	WR
0.00	0.00	0.00	0.00	0.00	0.15
0.00	0.00	0.00	0.00	0.00	1.90
3.19	0.52	0.00	0.00	0.00	1.66
79.02	6.85	0.85	0.00	0.00	4.40
4.28	85.93	8.29	0.73	0.62	0.15
0.00	3.50	87.18	2.09	3.89	3.34
0.00	0.52	28.18	53.12	18.18	0.00

Source: *Default and Recovery Rates of Corporate Bond Issuers*, Moody's, January 2006.

It should also be noted that historical models are dealing with "real" probabilities. Any pricing based on this type of model needs to incorporate a risk-adjusted cost of capital.

Statistical Models

Statistical models (credit scores) use various descriptive criteria, such as financial ratios and economic factors, which are given weightings such that the sum of the weighted values can be compared to a scale to determine credit quality.

In general, the form is

$$Score = \sum_{i=1}^{N} W_i R_i$$

where

Wi is the weight for risk factor I, and
R_i is the risk factor.

This usually is an attempt to automate a skilled analyst's thought process. Examples of factors include

❏ Profitability
❏ Leverage
❏ Growth
❏ Liquidity
❏ Factors to capture credit cycle

These systems are usually created using advanced regression techniques and require frequent revalidation via back-testing.

Example: Consumer Lending Criteria

CRITERIA	POINTS
Unemployed	–
Employed	+1
At current employer for more than two years	+3
Owns home	+2
Other	

Based on the applicant's characteristics, the points are simply summed up and if the total is greater than 17, the applicant is approved for a credit card.

This technique is best suited to large homogenous portfolios, such as consumer loans, but is also applied to individual firms (for example, to generate shadow ratings—ratings S&P or Moody's might give to an entity if they were to rate them):

CRITERIA	WEIGHTING
Asset/Liability ratio	1.3
EBITDA/Sales ratio	.0
Other	

Structural Models

The most common structural model of default is that of Merton.[1] Merton treats equity as a call option on the assets of a firm where the strike price is the level of the liabilities. When the value of the assets goes below the value of the liabilities, the option holder does not exercise the right to the assets and allows the option to expire (that is, the option holder defaults and hands over the assets to the liability holders). Therefore, if the components of a firm (assets, liabilities, and equity) are known, a probability of default can be inferred. (See **FIGURE 8.9**.)

The value of the equity and its volatility are directly observable in the marketplace. Therefore, this is considered a "market-driven" model. Structural models are very appealing as they attempt to model the "real world" as closely as desired. They also have many moving parts and can yield rich dynamics. Their main drawback is that they can be hard to use in practice

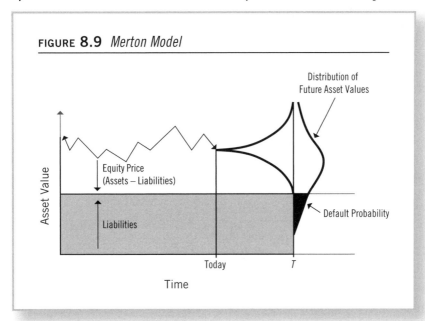

FIGURE 8.9 *Merton Model*

Distribution of Future Asset Values

Asset Value

Equity Price (Assets – Liabilities)

Liabilities

Default Probability

Today

T

Time

and struggle to match the market. One classic example of this for the original Merton model is that the assets of the company evolve continuously over time and as such, there is no chance of a "surprise" default. Implied short-term credit spreads are, therefore, zero for this type of model.

There have been many attempts at improving and expanding the original Merton model with mixed success. These include adding jumps in the asset value or adding a "fuzzier" definition of the default boundary.

KMV is the best-known implementation of the Merton model.

KMV uses a proprietary process and database to calculate an EDF. In broad terms, KMV uses the Merton model to calculate the number of standard deviations a company is from default (termed the distance to default). The distance to default is then compared against a historical database of observed defaults to find out how many similar companies with a similar distance to default actually defaulted. This mapped historical observed default frequency is then published as the EDF.

It should be noted that this model is also based on historical (and hence real) probabilities of default. Any pricing based on this model needs to incorporate a risk-adjusted cost of capital.

Reduced-Form Models

In reduced-form models, a particular dynamic is mathematically modeled in a way that allows calibration to observed market prices. The particular dynamic modeled may not necessarily be anything that is observable in the market. The basic idea is to come up with a model that provides enough flexibility and dynamics to calibrate and match what is observed in the market. The choice of what is modeled typically is a matter of mathematical convenience.

Reduced-form models are common in derivative pricing and are the same class of model used in interest-rate and equity derivative pricing. In those markets it may be typical to model the overnight interest rate or the stock price. In the credit markets it is typical to model the hazard rate or credit spread.

Reduced-form models have a number of advantages and tend to be the model of choice for mark-to-market, pricing, and hedging applications. Advantages include:

❑ Focused on the essential feature of interest
❑ Very few parameters make it easy to see what impact changing the parameters may have
❑ Easy to work with numerically

The disadvantage of reduced-form models is that they may be missing real-world features and the parameters may be difficult to interpret.

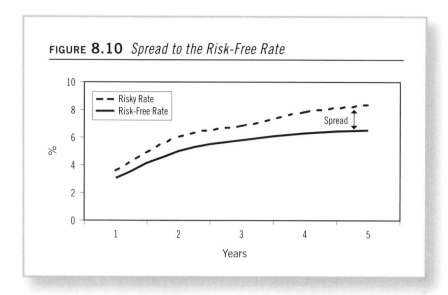

FIGURE **8.10** *Spread to the Risk-Free Rate*

Spread-Based Models

One type of reduced-form credit model is based on modeling credit spreads. There are several choices for what spreads to model. One possibility is to model the yield spread between corporate bonds and treasury bonds.

It should be noted that the spread to the treasury, or risk-free rate, incorporates the credit-risk premium as well as any liquidity premium. The credit-risk premium includes a probability of default and a recovery assumption.

Spread models are appealing for a number of reasons including the fact that the parameters (spreads) are observable in the market and historical data exists to simplify calibration. One negative is the difficulty of incorporating and calibrating the likelihood of a sudden default (rather than just incremental spread movements).

As a simple example, look at the relationship between zero-coupon corporate bond prices, the probability of default, and the recovery rate.

Assume that the liquidity premium is not significant. Zero-coupon prices are used for simplicity (not typically observable in the market and, therefore, are derived from the yield curves—via "bootstrapping").

Risky zero price = Risk-free zero price × [(1 – *PD*) + (*PD* × REC)]

where
  probability of default (*PD*) is between 0 and 1, and
  recovery assumption (REC) is between 0 and 1.

Example A: *PD* = 0, therefore, it is risk-free:

Risky zero price = Risk-free zero price
= Risk-free zero price × [(1 – 0) + (0 × REC)]

Example B: *PD* = 1, therefore, it has defaulted:

Risky zero price = REC value
= Risk-free zero price × [(1 – 1) + (1 × REC)]

Example C: Everything in between

The following formula gives a rough approximation:

$$PD = \frac{S}{1 - R}$$

where

PD = probability of default
S = risky versus risk-free price spread of zero-coupon bonds
R = recovery assumption as a decimal
See **FIGURE 8.11**.

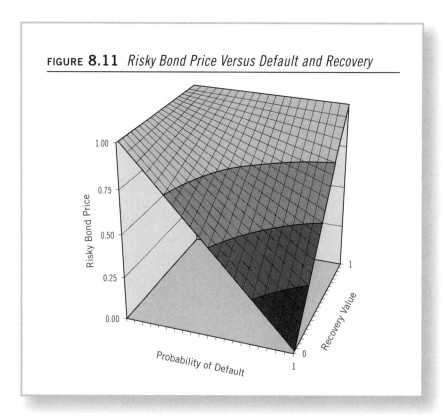

FIGURE **8.11** *Risky Bond Price Versus Default and Recovery*

Example: Assume recovery value = 40%

	ONE-YEAR ZERO RATE	PRICE
Risk-free	2.00	98.039
Risky	3.25	96.852
Spread		1.187
$PD = 1.98\%$		

Hazard-Rate Models

Hazard-rate models are borrowed directly from engineering's failure analysis. Default is taken as a random event in time modeled as the first event of a Poisson process governed by a default intensity $\lambda(u)$.

The probability of a default happening before time T, $P(T)$ is

$$P(T) = 1 - e^{\int_0^T -\lambda(u)du}$$

The default intensity is then the probability of default over the next instant (given no default has occurred).

Intuitively the hazard rate is simply the short-term probability of default. The use of the hazard rate is simply to facilitate a mathematical framework

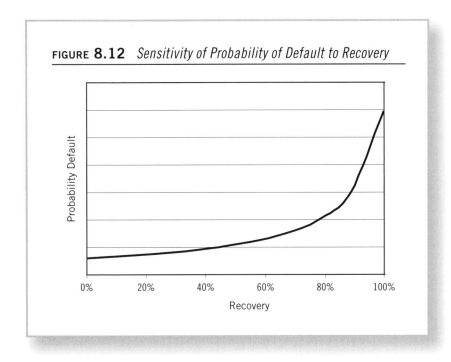

FIGURE **8.12** *Sensitivity of Probability of Default to Recovery*

that is familiar to interest-rate derivatives. Compare this to the typical form of the discount factor (DF) given the short rate $r(t)$.

$$DF\left(T\right) = e^{\int\limits_0^T -r(t)dt}$$

The market standard is to use a deterministic step function for $\lambda(u)$, which is calibrated to CDS quotes.

In this chapter, we have just touched the surface of the broad subject of credit modeling. Following chapters will elaborate on hazard-rate modeling and outline common market practice for pricing credit default swaps and collateralized debt obligations.

Chapter Notes

1. R. C. Merton, "On the Pricing of Corporate Debt: The Risk Structure of Interest Rates," _Journal of Finance_ 29 (1974): 449–470.

CHAPTER 9

CDS Valuation

SANTA FEDERICO, ANDREA PETRELLI,
JUN ZHANG, AND VIVEK KAPOOR

W̲e start with terminology widely used to describe a single-name CDS. To focus on the basic risk concepts, we work with an idealized continuous payment case without addressing the term structure of interest rates or credit spreads.

Symbol and Units	Description
$r\,[1/t]$	Default, risk-free interest rate
$T\,[t]$	Maturity of bond or CDS
$N[\$]$	Notional
$s\,[1/t]$	Spread over risk-free rate paid to risky bond investor
$\hat{s}\,[1/t]$	Continuous CDS spread paid by purchaser of default protection
R	Fraction of notional recovered in the event of default
$\lambda[1/t]$	Risk-neutral default hazard rate
$f_{t_d}(\tau\,\vert\,\lambda)[1/t]$	Risk-neutral probability density function of time to default
$F_{t_d}(\tau\,\vert\,\lambda)$	Cumulative risk-neutral probability density function of time to default
$PV01(r,T)[t]$	Present value of a unit continuous no-default coupon stream received over $t\in[0,\ T]$
$RPV01(r,\lambda,T)[t]$	Risk-neutral expectation of the present value of a unit continuous defaultable coupon stream received over $t\in[0,\ T]$, using r as the discount rate
$Dmtm(r,\lambda,T)$	Risk-neutral expectation of the present value of pay-

ments made by protection seller, using r as the discount rate

$Pmtm(r, \lambda, T)$ — Risk-neutral expectation of the present value of premiums to be paid by protection purchaser, using r as the discount rate

mtm — Protection sellers' mark-to-market of the CDS

$cbv(s, r, \lambda, T)$ — Risk-neutral expectation of the present value of payments made to a bond investor. The hazard rate can be calibrated by equating this to the price of the bond. The market practice is to mark CDS spreads assuming the existence of a bond that trades at par.

$CS01$ — The change in the CDS mtm due to a 1 bp increase of s

$DV01$ — The change in the CDS mtm due to a 1 bp increase in r

$RR01$ — The change in the CDS mtm due to a 1% increase in R

VOD — The P&L impact of the issuer defaulting

$$f_{t_d}(\tau \mid \lambda) = \lambda e^{-\lambda \tau}; \ F_{t_d}(\tau \mid \lambda) = 1 - e^{-\lambda \tau} \tag{9.1}$$

$$PV01(r, T) = \int_0^T e^{-rt} dt = \frac{1 - e^{-rT}}{r} \tag{9.2}$$

$$RPV01(r, \lambda, T) = PV01(r, T) \int_T^\infty f_{t_d}(\tau \mid \lambda) d\tau + \int_0^T PV01(r, \tau) f_{t_d}(\tau \mid \lambda) d\tau =$$

$$PV01(r, T) e^{-\lambda T} + \left(\frac{\lambda}{r}\right) [PV01(\lambda, T) - PV01(r + \lambda, T)] = PV01(r + \lambda, T) \tag{9.3}$$

That $RPV01(r, \lambda, T) = PV01(r + \lambda, T)$ is an expression of the common practice of accounting for credit risk by discounting based on the "risky curve."

$$Dmtm(r, \lambda, T) = \int_0^T N(1 - R) e^{-rr} f_{t_d}(\tau \mid \lambda) d\tau = N(1 - R) \lambda RPV01(r, \lambda, T) \tag{9.4}$$

$$Pmtm(r, \lambda, T) = sRPV01(r, \lambda, T) N \tag{9.5}$$

$$cbv(s,r,\lambda,T) = N\Big[(s+r)RPV01(r,\lambda,T) + e^{-rT}e^{-\lambda T} + R\lambda RPV01(r,T)\Big]$$

$$= \Big\{e^{-(\lambda+r)T} + RPV01(r,\lambda,T)\times[s+r+R\lambda]\Big\}$$

$$= \Big\{1 + RPV01(r,\lambda,T)\times[s-\lambda(1-R)]\Big\}N \qquad (9.6)$$

$$cbv(s,r,\lambda,T) = N \Rightarrow s = \lambda(1-R) \qquad (9.7)$$

At the pricing date, the swap spread is intentioned to equate the premium leg *mtm* (9.5) to the contingent payment leg *mtm* (9.4) assuming the existence of a bond that trades at par (9.7):

$$Pmtm(r,\lambda,T) = Dmtm(r,\lambda,T) \Rightarrow s = s \qquad (9.8)$$

Subsequent movements in the spread *s* result in *mtm* movements of the swap:

$$mtm(t) = Pmtm(r,\lambda,T) - Dmtm(r,\lambda,T)$$

$$= [s(0) - s(t)]\times RPV01(r,\lambda,T)\times N \qquad (9.9)$$

In (9.9), $s(0)$ is the premium of the CDS contract that started at $t = 0$, the current break-even swap spread is $s(t)$, and (9.7) relates the swap spread to the risk-neutral hazard rate.

Based on (9.6) and (9.9), the price of the reference cash bond, which was at par at the time the swap was priced, is related to the swap *mtm* and notional as follows:

$$cbv(s,r,\lambda,T) = N + mtm \qquad (9.10)$$

As a result, the bond equivalent market value of a CDS can be invoked and is given by (9.10), which is the value of the bond that was at par when the CDS contract was entered into. Such a bond equivalent has the same spread and interest rate sensitivity as the CDS.

With greater notational complexity, (9.1) through (9.10) can be expressed for term-dependent, risk-free rates, spreads, and hazard rates, and discrete payment intervals, as is the case for standard CDS *mtm* modeling.

High-yield CDS are often quoted in terms of upfront payment rather than spreads. This is consistent with the observation of high-yield bonds often trading on price.

The $RPV01$ can be thought of as a risky duration over which premiums are paid and default occurs. Therefore, the mtm of the premium leg is simply a product of the swap spread and risky duration (9.5), and the mtm of the contingent leg is the payoff $N \times (1 - R)$ multiplied by the effective probability of default over the risky duration (9.6).

The commonly used risk sensitivity $CS01$ is the change in mtm of the CDS due to a unit change in spread (typically 1 bp/year):

$$CS01 \equiv$$
$$\equiv mtm|_{s+1/10000} - mtm|_s$$
$$= N \times \left\{ \left[s(0) - \left(s + \frac{1}{1000} \right) \right] RPV01(r, \lambda', T) - [s(0) - s] RPV01(r, \lambda, T) \right\}$$

(9.11)

where
$$\lambda' = \frac{s + 1/10000}{1 - R}; \qquad \lambda = \frac{s}{1 - R}$$

The linear (in spread) approximation of (9.11) that ignores the change in the risky duration due to a change in the spread by 1 bp is

$$CS01 \approx -RPV01(r, \lambda, T) \times \frac{N}{10000}$$

(9.12)

For a CDS protection purchaser, the sign in (9.12) needs to be changed to positive (that is, an mtm gain occurs if spreads widen by 1 bp).

The interest-rate sensitivity of the CDS mtm is described by the $DV01$:

$$DV01 = [s(0) - s(t)] \times \left\{ RPV01(r + 1/10000, \lambda, T) - RPV01(r, \lambda, T) \right\} \times N$$

(9.13)

The recovery-rate sensitivity of the mtm arises due to the dependence of $RPV01$ on recovery (via the relationship of hazard rates and recovery for a given credit spread):

$$RR01 = [s(0) - s(t)] \times \left\{ RPV01(r, \lambda_{R+0.01}, T) - RPV01(r, \lambda_R, T) \right\} \times N$$

(9.14)

The P&L impact (on the seller of CDS protection) of default is assessed by netting the contingent cash-flow [that is, $-N \times (1 - R)$] and the elimination of the mtm that would occur after the position is closed:

$$VOD = -N \times (1 - R) - mtm \qquad (9.15)$$

Example 1

Key CDS variables for a fair CDS contract at inception (that is, $mtm = 0$ at trade date) $r = 0.035$ (1/yr); $T = 5$ yrs; $R = 0.3$; $PV01 = 4.59$ yr; $N = \$100$ mm; $VOD = -\$70$ mm

(BPS/YR)	λ (1/YR)	RPV01 (YRS)	CS01 ($MM)	DMTM ($MM)
20	0.0029	4.55	−0.0455	0.9
50	0.0071	4.51	−0.0451	2.3
100	0.0143	4.43	−0.0443	4.4
200	0.0286	4.28	−0.0428	8.6
500	0.0714	3.87	−0.0387	19.4
1000	0.1429	3.31	−0.0331	33.1

Example 2

Key CDS variables for a CDS contract as a function of changes in credit spreads $s(0) = 100$ bps; $r = 0.035$ (1/yr); $T = 5$ yrs; $R = 0.3$; $PV01 = 4.59$ yr; $N = \$100$ mm

S (BPS/YR)	DV01 ($MM/100)	CS01 ($MM)	RR01 ($MM)	MTM ($MM)	VOD ($MM)
20	−0.088	−0.0470	−0.0003	3.60	−73.6
50	−0.054	−0.0458	−0.0005	2.25	−72.3
100	0	−0.0443	0	0	−70.0
200	0.101	−0.0417	0.0040	−4.29	−65.7
500	0.353	−0.0337	0.0370	−15.51	−54.5
1000	0.636	−0.024	0.1310	−29.81	−40.2

CHAPTER 10

CDO Valuation

SANTA FEDERICO, ANDREA PETRELLI,
JUN ZHANG, AND VIVEK KAPOOR

W e employ here a latent variable framework, which accounts for default correlation by introducing common factors among the variables themselves. Two semianalytical approaches are described—namely Fourier transform and direct calculation of the convolution integral via a recursive method. We present the formulation in a loss continuum framework and later we briefly describe the mapping of relevant quantities after having discredited the loss support for numerical integration.

Default Mechanism

Define the latent variable $X_i = f(w)Z_i$, the normal standardized asset return Z_i has a systematic component and an idiosyncratic one ($Z_i = \sqrt{\rho}\, Z + \sqrt{1-\rho}\,\varepsilon_i$), w is an independent random variable, f a function. The pair-wise correlation between the drivers Z_i is $corr(Z_i, Z_j) = \rho + (1-\rho)\delta_{ij}$ considering one period default analysis. Within a time horizon (t), the obligor (i) defaults if the latent variable X_i falls below a threshold level determined by the cumulative risk-neutral default probability p_t^i:

$$X_i < \alpha_i;\; P(X_i < \alpha_i) \equiv H(\alpha_i) = p_t^i \Leftrightarrow \alpha_i = H^{-1}(p_t^i) \qquad (10.1)$$

which implies $Z_i < \alpha_i / f(w)$. The latent variable X_i triggers the default when it falls below the default threshold, which implies a stochastic threshold on the standardized asset return Z_i. The presence of the stochastic threshold models the incompleteness of information. The risk-neutral unconditional default probability p_t^i of the obligor i within the given time horizon t can be calibrated to the market by using quoted par CDS spread via standard root-finding routine. Conditional on the realization of the common factor, the probability of default is:

$$p_t(i \mid Z, w) = \Phi\left(\frac{H^{-1}(p_t^i) / f(w) - \sqrt{\rho}\, Z}{\sqrt{1-\rho}}\right) \qquad (10.2)$$

If w follows a x^2 with v degrees of freedom and $f(w) = \sqrt{v / w}$, then the Student-t copula is recovered. Within the previous framework, a Monte Carlo (MC) simulation seems to be the natural approach to achieve the distribution of the collateral loss. Nevertheless, MC needs variance reduction techniques given the tail feature of the events under analysis. In particular, the sensitivities at the individual obligor level show a high level of noise. Semianalytical techniques are preferable, reserving MC whenever exotic features prevent the achievement of closed form solutions. Here, we illustrate general techniques of portfolio loss aggregation applied in pricing of synthetic CDO tranches and the Gaussian copula, that is $f(w) = 1$, and only the conditioning on Z is needed.

Conditional Individual Loss Density

The previous expression allows us to obtain the conditional loss density for every single source of loss on the pool. In a fixed severity framework, the probability density of the obligor n within a time t conditional on Z follows:

$$L_t^n(x_n \mid Z) = (1 - p_t(n \mid Z))\delta(x_n) + p_t(n \mid Z)\delta(x_n - \lambda_n), \qquad (10.3)$$

where λ_n is the loss given default of the nth credit.

Conditional Portfolio Loss Density

Exploiting the conditional independence, the conditional portfolio loss PDF if given by the convolution of the loss conditional PDFs of the single underlying obligors:

$$H_t^N(x \mid Z) = \int \prod_{n=1}^{N} L_t^n(x_n \mid Z)\, \delta\left(\sum_{n-1}^{N} x_n - x\right) dx_1 \cdots dx_N \qquad (10.4)$$

This is the master equation of the conditional independence portfolio loss calculation. $H_t^N(x \mid Z)$ represents the loss probability density the portfolio on N obligors in a time t conditional on Z.

Convolution Integral of Conditional Portfolio Loss Density

Fourier Transform

The Fourier transform (FT) of the convolution of N functions equals the product of the FT of each function:

$$\tilde{H}_t^N(\omega \mid Z) = \prod_{n=1}^N \tilde{L}_t^n(\omega \mid Z) \tag{10.5}$$

$$H_t^N(x \mid Z) = \Im^{-1} \prod_{n=1}^N \tilde{L}_t^n(\omega \mid Z) \tag{10.6}$$

Direct Convolution by Recursion

The convolution integral (10.4) can be alternatively evaluated by recursion by noticing that:

$$H_t^N(x \mid Z) =$$
$$= \int L_t^N(x_N \mid Z)\delta(x - y - x_N)dx_N dy \int \prod_{n=1}^{N-1} L_t^n(x_n \mid Z)\delta(\sum_{n-1}^{N-1} x_n - y) \, dx_1 \cdots dx_{N-1}$$
$$\tag{10.7}$$

which integrating out the first Dirac delta yields

$$H_t^N(x \mid Z) = \int L_t^N(x_N \mid Z) H_t^{N-1}(x - x_N \mid Z) dx_N \tag{10.8}$$

with the boundary condition $H_t^1(x \mid Z) = L_t^1(x \mid Z)$. Once the conditional pool loss PDF has been obtained (either by recursion or FT), the final step is to integrate over the common factor(s) to get the unconditional portfolio loss PDF.

$$H_t^N(x) = \int_{-\infty}^{+\infty} H_t^N(x \mid Z)\phi(Z)dZ \tag{10.9}$$

Tranche Valuation

A CDO tranche is an option on the pool loss. Once the risk-neutral portfolio loss distribution is obtained, it is straightforward to get the value of any claim on the pool loss. The cash flow is in general a function of the collateral loss $f(L)$. In the case of a synthetic CDO tranche with a lower attachment A and an upper attachment B, the contingent payment equals the pool excess loss over the lower attachment but does not exceed the upper attachment:

$$\Lambda^{AB}(x) = \max(x - A, 0) - \max(x - B, 0) \tag{10.10}$$

where x represents the pool loss. Given the unconditional pool loss density and the above payoff allows us to define the tranche survival function:

$$S^{AB}(t) = 1 - \frac{1}{B - A} \int_0^{+\infty} \Lambda^{AB}(x) \, H_t^N(x) \, dx \tag{10.11}$$

Since the payoff is essentially a projector onto the layer [A, B] of the capital structure, the survival function represents the fractional erosion of the tranche notional within the time t. It is now straightforward to write the two legs of the synthetic CDO tranche.

Contingent Leg

$$V_{Def} = \sum_{k=1}^{P} (S^{AB}(t_{k-1}) - S^{AB}(t_k)) \, B(t_k) \tag{10.12}$$

Premium Leg

$$V_{Prm} = w \sum_{k=1}^{P} S^{AB}(t_k) \, B(t_k) \, (t_k - t_{k-1}), \tag{10.13}$$

where $B(t_k)$ is the discount factor.

Numerical Implementation

The numerical implementation of both the FT and the recursively direct convolution calculation requires dividing the loss space into a discrete number of loss buckets (M). After having defined a base dollar loss of the whole portfolio, any admissible portfolio loss x is binned into an integer representing the multiple of base. The calculation of the portfolio loss density is numerically achieved by using the following mapping into the discrete space:

CONTINUUM	DISCRETE
x_n	j_n
$p_t(n \mid Z)$	$p_t(n \mid Z)$
$L_t^n(x_n \mid Z)$	$L_t^n(j_n \mid Z)$
$H_t^N(x \mid Z)$	$H_t^N(j \mid Z)$
$\Lambda^{AB}(x)$	$\Lambda^{AB}(j)$

❏ j_n is an integer running from 0 to M-1 representing the multiple of base loss.
❏ $p_t(n \mid Z)$ is the conditional probability of default of the obligor n within a time period t.
❏ $L_t^n(j_n \mid Z)$ represents the conditional probability of the obligor n losing a multiple j_n of the base loss in a time t.
❏ $H_t^N(j \mid Z)$ is the conditional probability of the portfolio of N obligors losing a multiple j of the base loss in a time period t.
❏ $\Lambda^{AB}(j)$ is the synthetic CDO cash flow associated with a pool loss equal to j-times the base loss.

The formula (10.8) becomes:

$$H_t^N(j \mid Z) = \sum_{j_N=0}^{j} H_t^{N-1}(j - j_N \mid Z) L_t^N(j_N \mid Z) \quad (10.14)$$

with $H_t^1(j \mid Z) = L_t^1(j \mid Z)$. The Fourier integral becomes a Fourier series. A popular fast implementation of the Fourier series (FFT) requires the number of the loss buckets M to be equal to a power of 2. Once conditional, the portfolio loss density has been achieved (either via direct convolution or via FT), standard numerical quadrature routines allow effective integration over the common factors. The recursion method turns out to be considerably faster than the FFT algorithm.

Compound and Base Correlation

The equation (10.10) embeds the correlation dependence through the conditional default probability. The correlation is a key parameter that shapes the distribution of the collateral loss. Taking a view on the correlation amounts to taking a view on the shape of the collateral loss distribution. In particular, investors can bet on realization of extreme losses (typically driven by systemic factors) by buying super-senior protection. This position is an indirect long position on the tail of the distribution of the collateral loss. Unfortunately, the relationship between correlation and tranche spread (cost of protection) is not always unambiguous.

By noticing that $\Lambda^{AB}(x) = \Lambda^{0B}(x) - \Lambda^{0A}(x)$, the integral appearing in equation (10.11) can be written in the following fashion:

$$\int_0^{+\infty} \Lambda^{AB}(x) H_t^N(x, \rho_{AB})\, dx = \int_0^{+\infty} \left(\Lambda^{0B}(x) - \Lambda^{0A}(x)\right)\, H_t^N(x, \rho_{AB})\, dx$$

where the correlation dependence in the portfolio loss density has been made explicit. Now, we write the previous equation as follows:

$$\int_0^{+\infty} \left(\Lambda^{0B}(x) - \Lambda^{0A}(x)\right)\, H_t^N(x, \rho_{AB})\, dx$$
$$= \int_0^{+\infty} \Lambda^{0B}(x)\, H_t^N(x, \rho_{0B})\, dx - \int_0^{+\infty} \Lambda^{0A}(x)\, H_t^N(x, \rho_{0A})\, dx \tag{10.15}$$

The equation (10.15) is the definition of the base correlation. Base correlation is the correlation of an equity tranche. In other words, the correlation is assumed to be dependent on the tranche strikes. Based on the previous equation, a single tranche is priced *using two correlation parameters rather than one*. Suppose the spread of the tranches [A,B] and [0,A] are observed in the market. Then ρ_{0B} and ρ_{AB} can be directly backed out by using equation (10.15) [notice that $\Lambda^{00}(x) = 0$]. Then the equation (10.15) provides the recipe to back out the parameter ρ_{0B}. The situation is very similar to the interest-rate compounding. Given a variable Y, if there exists a metric (defined by a function f) such as

$$f(Y_{AB}) = f(Y_{0B}) - f(Y_{0A}) \tag{10.16}$$

then a compounding mechanism is defined. For example, for the rates:

$$f(R_{AB}) = R_{AB}(T_B - T_A)$$

and for the correlation:

$$f(\rho_{AB}) = \int_0^{+\infty} \Lambda^{AB}(x) H_t^N(x, \rho_{AB})\, dx$$

The compounding rule follows directly from equation (10.16), yielding the equation (10.15). The compounding mechanism suggests a calibration procedure based on a bootstrapping paradigm.

References

Brigham, E. O. (1988). *The Fast Fourier Transform and its Applications*, Upper Saddle River, NJ: Prentice Hall.

Embrechts, P., et al. (1999). Correlation and dependence in risk management: Properties and pitfalls. *Risk management: value at risk and beyond*, edited by M. Dempster. Cambridge: Cambridge University Press.

Frey, R, and McNeil A. J. (2003). Dependent defaults in models of portfolio credit risk. *Journal of Risk*, 6(1): 59–92 and references therein.

Jarrow, R. and Turnbull, S. (1995). Pricing derivatives on financial securities subject to credit risk. *Journal of Finance* 50(1), 53–85.

Lehman Brothers. *Fixed Income Quantitative Research Quarterly*. Volume 2004–Q4/Q4.

Li, D. (2000). On default correlation: A copula function Approach. RiskMetrics Group, working paper.

Merton, R. C. (1974). On the pricing of corporate debt: The risk structure of interest rates. *Journal of Finance* 29: 449–470.

Panjer, H. H. (1981). Recursive evaluation of a family of compound distributions. *ASTIN Bulletin* 12, 22–26.

Schönbucher, P. J. and Schubert D. (2001). Copula-dependent default risk in intensity models. Bonn University.

Wang, S. (1998). Aggregation of correlated risk portfolio: Models and algorithms. *Proceedings of the Casualty Actuarial Society* LXXXV: 848–939.

CHAPTER 11

Credit Derivative Products

PETER RIVERA

This chapter provides an overview of the characteristics, terms, and concepts associated with credit derivative transactions. It is hoped that the information in this chapter will help the reader who is new to credit derivatives more easily understand the applications described in the rest of this book.

Credit Derivative Defined

A commonly used definition of a credit derivative is: *A financial contract where the value is derived from an underlying market value incorporating credit risk.*

This definition is somewhat problematical in that it could be interpreted to encompass bond options, a product that has been around a long time and is usually not considered a credit derivative, or it could be interpreted to exclude asset swaps. Agreement on what is or isn't a credit derivative has only two practical implications:

1 **Statistics:** Different surveys include different products and, therefore, may not be directly comparable.
2 **Policies:** Effective risk management within a firm requires a common accepted definition to determine which internal controls apply.

The credit derivative market is characterized by a high degree of rapid innovation with new products and variations constantly being introduced. Nonetheless, credit derivatives can be grouped into three broad categories:

1 Single-name products (for example, asset swaps, total return swaps, credit default swaps (CDS), credit linked notes)
2 Multiname (portfolio) products (for example, first-to-default baskets)
3 Structured products (for example, collateralized debt obligations)

Asset Swaps

An asset swap is a package containing:

❑ A purchase of a bond
❑ An interest-rate swap that converts the bond's cash flows into a floating rate

Basic Mechanics

Counterparty (Ctpy) B purchases a bond, usually at par and usually from the same counterparty as the swap (Ctpy A in this example).

Ctpy B enters into a swap paying the bond coupon rate to Ctpy A and receiving a floating rate (see **FIGURE 11.1**).

In a generic asset swap, a fixed-rate bond's cash flows are exchanged for floating-rate cash flows. The floating-rate cash flows are determined using standard swap valuation methodology, such that the present value of the floating-rate payments equals the present value of the fixed-rate payments plus the difference between the market value of the bond and the price at which it was sold (usually par).

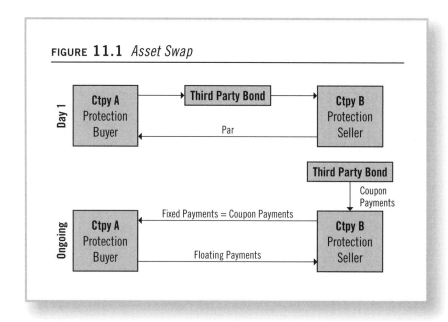

FIGURE **11.1** *Asset Swap*

However, the asset swap structure is very flexible and can, for example, convert the cash flows into a second currency and/or strip out an option component of the bond in order to meet the purchaser's needs.

It is very important to note that the purchaser (Ctpy B) must make all the fixed-rate payments to Ctpy A regardless of the performance of the bond.

What Was Achieved?

The seller (Ctpy A) no longer owns the bond and has no further exposure to it. Ctpy A now has a swap with Ctpy B and, therefore, has credit risk to it.

The purchaser (Ctpy B) owns the bond with the interest-rate risk neutralized (that is, Ctpy B has only the credit risk of the bond). They also have credit risk to Ctpy A on the swap.

There is some debate as to whether or not an asset swap should be considered a credit derivative or not. Essentially, Ctpy A achieves credit protection by selling the bond: there is nothing new in that. The swap merely facilitates the sale by making the bond's cash flows conform to the needs of the purchaser.

What is important, however, is that by artificially creating a corporate floating-rate bond, the credit default premium can be benchmarked as a spread to Libor. This is known as the par asset swap rate.

Recap

Risk transfer	Default
Balance sheet	Bond: on for purchaser (Ctpy B)
	Swap: off
Funding	Ctpy B must fund the bond purchase.
Transaction credit risk	Ctpy A and Ctpy B have credit risk to each other for the swap.

Primary Application
- Yield

Total Return Swaps

A *total return swap* (also known as a *total rate of return swap*) is a bilateral, off-balance-sheet transaction whereby the total economic performance of an asset is transferred in exchange for a periodic interest payment.

Basic Mechanics

Ctpy A is taking an artificial short position in the *reference asset*. The reference asset is typically either a bond or a loan but can also be an index.

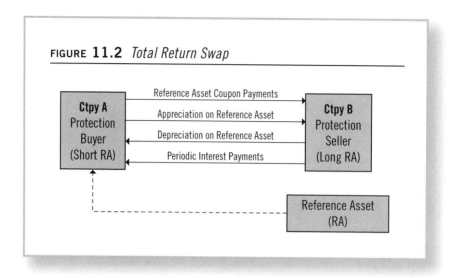

FIGURE **11.2** *Total Return Swap*

(Insofar as Ctpy A is laying off the downside risk of the reference asset, it is labeled as the protection buyer.) Typically, Ctpy A would own the reference asset; however, this is not a requirement of the transaction.

Ctpy B (sometimes referred to as the *investor*) is taking an artificial long position in the reference asset.

Therefore:

❑ Ctpy A must make payments to Ctpy B for the reference asset coupon payments and any appreciation in the value of the reference asset,

❑ Ctpy B must make payments to Ctpy A for any depreciation in the value of the reference asset and periodic interest payments, which repre-

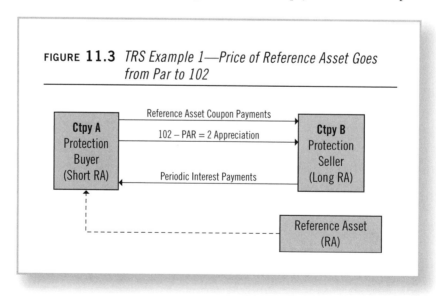

FIGURE **11.3** *TRS Example 1—Price of Reference Asset Goes from Par to 102*

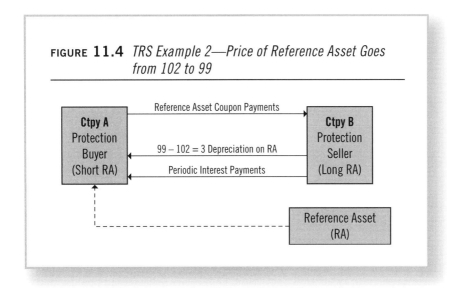

FIGURE 11.4 *TRS Example 2—Price of Reference Asset Goes from 102 to 99*

sent the funding of the position and are typically expressed as a spread to Libor (see **FIGURE 11.2**).

Payments for appreciation/depreciation are made either periodically (for example, semiannually on the coupon dates) or at the end of the transaction (typically for short-term trades). See **FIGURES 11.3** and **11.4**.

Applications

Funding

Between two counterparties, the counterparty with the lower funding cost will likely be the protection buyer and short the reference asset (Ctpy A in our example):

Assume that Ctpy A's funding cost is Libor −10 and Ctpy B's is Libor +20. In this situation, Ctpy B will likely be happy to receive the return of the reference asset via a TRS as long as it is sufficiently lower than their funding cost of +20. For example, they may enter into a TRS whereby Ctpy A pays Ctpy B the return on the reference asset in exchange for payments of Libor +15.

Ctpy B has picked up 5 bps; clearly, they should be happy (assuming that they conclude that this compensates them for the additional credit risk of Ctpy A). Additionally, the TRS is not reflected on their balance sheet.

But what is in it for Ctpy A? Ctpy A is now earning 25 bps (+15 from Ctpy B + their 10 bps sub-Libor funding) on an asset whose probability of default is a function of both the reference asset and Ctpy B: they will only incur a loss if Ctpy B defaults and cannot make a payment upon default of the reference asset. Assuming anything less than 100% correlation between the reference asset and Ctpy B should result in a probability of default lower than either the reference asset or Ctpy B. Effectively, they will be earning a higher return relative to the riskiness of the transaction.

Regulatory Capital Management

Under the current BIS international regulatory capital guidelines, banks are required to hold capital equal to 8% of risk-weighted assets.[1] Risk-weighted assets are determined according to the following scheme:

❑ Sovereign debt of OECD countries receives 0% risk weighting (that is, no capital is required).

❑ Senior debt of banks from OECD countries receives 20% risk weighting (that is, 1.6% capital required: 20% × 8%).

❑ Non-OECD banks and corporate debt receive 100% risk weighting (that is, 8% capital is required).

Under this scheme, if a bank wants to hold $1 million of XYZ Company bonds directly, it will have to hold $8 million of capital. However, if it chooses to establish an artificial long position in the XYZ bonds via a TRS from an OECD bank, it will only have to hold $1.6 million of regulatory capital.

Regulatory capital rules are complex, and a complete treatment of this important topic is beyond the scope of this chapter. However, several points are worth noting:

❑ Individual countries are free to modify the BIS guidelines when implementing them within their jurisdiction so the efficacy of the TRS (or credit derivative in general) as a source of regulatory capital relief may vary from country to country.

❑ A revision of the guidelines known as Basel II has been under development for many years and is expected to be in force within the next few years.

❑ Within the United States, the treatment of credit derivatives differs between the banking book and the trading book:

—*Within the banking book*, writing or assuming credit risk is considered a direct credit substitute with the entire notional amount placed in the risk category of the reference asset or the counterparty, whichever is higher. The purchase of credit protection will receive capital relief if it meets specific guidelines that include: it must be explicit, irrevocable, unconditional, and cover the full term of the underlying asset.

—*Within the trading book*, credit derivatives are treated as underlying cash instruments for purposes of VaR model analysis of general market and specific risk. Additionally, they are subject to counterparty risk-based capital charges, which are a function of the credit quality of the reference asset.

Leverage

If an investor wants exposure to an asset, achieving it by direct purchase would require funding the full amount. Using a TRS would provide significant leverage. The amount of leverage will be a function of how much collateral is required to be posted. Due to the credit risk inherent in a TRS, it is the practice for the weaker of the counterparties, typically the counterparty artificially long the reference asset, to post collateral to protect against adverse movements in the transaction. In a typical case of 5% of notional, an investor can use a TRS to leverage his position twenty times versus an outright purchase.

Increased Access to Asset Classes

Investments in some securities can be achieved more easily through a TRS than through a direct purchase (for example, foreign market securities, investments in market sectors via index trades, and loans by nontraditional loan holders, for example, hedge funds).

TRSs are sometimes used by investors who are seeking exposure to noninvestment-grade assets but require an investment-grade counterparty.

Other Applications

❑ The maturity of the TRS can be shorter than the maturity of the underlying reference asset, thereby providing the ability to create "new asset classes."

❑ Lenders can transfer loan risk more easily than through assignment, without the borrower's permission or knowledge and still retain ownership rights.

❑ Taxes can be deferred by eliminating economic risk to an asset without selling it.

❑ TRSs provide a mechanism to establish a short position in securities that are otherwise unavailable in the borrow market.

Recap

Risk transfer	Total return
Balance sheet	Off
Funding	Via periodic appreciation/depreciation payments and collateral
Transaction credit risk	Ctpy A and Ctpy B have credit risk to each other for the swap.

Primary Applications

- Funding
- Bank regulatory capital management
- Leverage
- Access

Credit Default Swaps and Options

CDSs and options are the most common form of credit derivative transaction, accounting for 50% of the outstanding transactions.[2] The current standard CDS is for a term of five years and is the basis for the index products that will be discussed later in this chapter.

CDSs and options are often described as insurance contracts against the default of a defined entity. This is a somewhat simplified interpretation, as will be discussed in more detail later in this section.

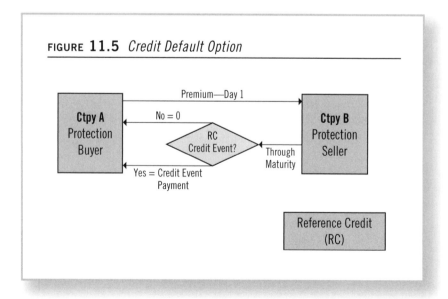

FIGURE 11.5 *Credit Default Option*

Basic Mechanics

Credit Default Option

As shown in **FIGURE 11.5**, Ctpy A, the *protection buyer* (also referred to as the *fixed-rate payer*) pays a premium at inception of the trade.

Ctpy B, *the protection seller* (also referred to as the *floating-rate payer*) makes a *credit event payment* if there is a *credit event* on the *reference credit*.

Credit Default Swap

A credit default swap is essentially the same as a credit default option with the primary difference being that whereas in the option the premium is paid up front, in the swap the premium is paid via periodic payments, usually quarterly expressed as a number of basis points (see **FIGURE 11.6**).

Ctpy A, the protection buyer (also referred to as the fixed-rate payer) pays a premium through periodic interest payments (typically expressed in basis points).

Ctpy B, the protection seller (also referred to as the floating-rate payer) makes a credit event payment if there is a credit event on the reference credit.

CDSs and options are very similar in that the protection bought and sold is the same if held to maturity. However, insofar as the mechanism for paying the premium is different (up front for the option and over time for the swap), they will have the following differences:

❑ The valuation will be different if unwound prior to maturity.

❑ An option premium payment requires up-front funding.

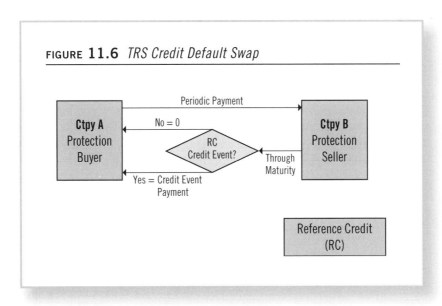

FIGURE 11.6 *TRS Credit Default Swap*

❏ The protection seller's credit risk to the protection buyer differs:
   —*Option:* there is no credit risk once the premium has been paid.
   —*Swap:* the protection seller has risk to the protection buyer insofar as should the buyer default prior to maturity, the protection seller may not be able to replace the transaction at the same (or better) rate.

The Devil Is in the Details and the Details Are in the Documentation

So far, we have determined that by paying a premium, the protection buyer expects to receive a *payment* if a *credit* has a *credit event*. (The credit event is usually interpreted as a default.) However, the specifics of the transaction must be spelled out in the documentation.

Virtually all CDS and option trades now use the ISDA credit derivative documentation,[3] which provides standardized terminology and terms. In addition to the standard ISDA swap terminology (such as effective dates, counterparties, notional amounts, and so on), credit default swap documentation addresses three critical questions:

1 What is the *credit event payment?*
2 On what (or who) is the credit protection being bought or sold?
3 When does a *credit event payment* need to be made?

What Is the Credit Event Payment?

If a payment must be made, there are three possibilities:

1 *Fixed amount (for example, $10 million).* This is a form of digital option (that is, the payout is not affected by the severity of the credit event in terms of the losses on the reference entity's obligations). This technique was more common in the early days of the credit derivatives market, became less common as the market developed, and recently has been revived as a technique for addressing recovery rate risk (see the recovery rate swap discussion that follows).

2 *Physical delivery.* The protection buyer delivers obligations of the reference credit (loans or bonds subject to the defined deliverable obligations, as described later) with a face value equal to the notional amount of the trade to the protection seller, who pays par for them.

3 *Cash settled.* Rather than deliver a bond or loan, a cash payment is made by the protection seller to the protection buyer equal to

$$(\text{Par} - \text{Default value}) \times \text{Notional amount of trade}$$

where the default value is determined by a dealer poll of prices for the deliverable obligation.

On What (or Who) Is the Credit Protection Being Bought or Sold?

The following are the key terms for determining on what (or who) the credit default protection is being bought:

❑ *Reference entity* is the entity on which the credit protection is being bought or sold. Rules govern corporate restructurings (mergers and spin-offs).

❑ *Reference obligation* is a security used as a benchmark for the seniority of the *deliverable obligation.*

❑ *Obligations* defines which obligations can trigger a *credit event,* for example,

— borrowed money (which would include loans, bonds, deposits, and so on),

— bonds and/or loans, or

— specific obligations (for example, the 5% bonds due March 15, 2025).

❑ *Deliverable obligations* defines what can be delivered by the protection buyer for physical delivery or for determining loss/recovery value for cash settled trades (for example, bond or loan, currency, maximum maturity, and the like—subject to restructuring provisions discussed later).

Together, these parameters will define the universe of obligations from which the cheapest-to-deliver security will be determined. The more broadly it is defined, the greater the value of the protection and the higher the cost.

When Does a Credit Event Payment Have to Be Made?

In order to initiate a payment, the credit protection buyer must deliver a credit event notice to the calculation agent that states that a credit event has occurred and a notice of publicly available information naming the sources where the event is described.

Publicly available information sources would include the *Wall Street Journal,* the *Financial Times,* the Bloomberg Professional service, Dow Jones Telerate, and the like.

A notice of intended physical settlement must also be delivered stating what deliverable obligation will be delivered.

Credit events are negotiable but commonly include the following:

For corporations:

❑ *Bankruptcy*

❑ *Failure to pay*—subject to a threshold defined by the payment requirement. This threshold is in place to ensure that the failure to pay is sufficiently large and that a true credit event has occurred due to a deterioration of the credit quality of the reference credit.

❑ **Restructuring**—subject to a threshold defined by the default requirement. Restructuring has been one of the most contentious criteria for market participants to agree on. The 2003 *ISDA Credit Default Definitions* has four standard options:

 1 *Full*—a restructuring occurs when there is
    —A reduction in interest or principal.
    —Delay in interest payments or extension of maturity.
    —The reference obligation is subordinated.
    —This restructuring must be the result of a deterioration in credit quality.

 2 *Modified restructuring* (ModR)—same definition as full, however, the deliverable obligation is limited to a maximum maturity and must be fully transferable.

 3 *Modified modified restructuring* (ModModR)—similar to ModR, however, the deliverable obligation can have a longer maturity than the restructured security and allows for conditional transferability.

 4 *No restructuring*—credit event is subject only to bankruptcy and failure to pay.

❑ **Cross acceleration/Cross default**—due to reasons other than failure to pay (for example, breach of a loan covenant). This provision is not commonly included.

For sovereigns:
❑ **Repudiation**
❑ **Moratorium**

Repudiation and moratorium must be followed by either a failure to pay or a restructuring within the later of sixty days or the next coupon payment date of the reference obligation.

The more broadly the credit event is defined, the greater the protection and the higher the cost.

Valuation/Trading Price. As with credit derivatives in general, the valuation of CDSs or options is dependent on primarily two parameters: probability of default and recovery assumption. Ultimately, the price the trade is actually done at will be determined by supply and demand. Nonetheless, the price will generally be somewhere around the asset swap spread.

If the CDS spread is lower than the asset swap spread, it is said to have negative basis, and it would make sense to buy the asset swap and buy the protection.

If the CDS spread is higher than the asset swap spread, it is said to have positive basis, and it would make sense to sell the protection and sell the asset swap.

Positive basis is the norm (that is, the CDS spread is greater than the asset swap spread).

Possible reasons include:

- ❏ Shorting the bond/asset swap may be expensive or impossible.
- ❏ The CDS's events of default may be broader than bankruptcy and failure to pay.
- ❏ There is a premium due to the cheapest-to-deliver option.
- ❏ The bond is trading at a discount.

Credit Default Swaps/Options Versus Insurance

As stated at the beginning of this section, credit default swaps/options are somewhat analogous to an insurance contract. Such insurance contracts have been available long before credit derivatives were developed (though expensive and rare) typically from insurance companies. By the nature of their business, insurance companies are natural sellers of protection in the credit derivatives market.[4] However, there are a number of differences—the most significant being the certainty of the amount and timing of credit event payment. In an insurance contract, the insurer will make principal and interest payments on the established payment dates. In a CDS, there is a single payment sometime shortly after the credit event, and the exact amount is not known until shortly before the payment is due (unless the credit event payment is a fixed amount).

Applications

Applications of credit default swaps/options are very similar to those of total return swaps. However, it is more of a pure credit play insofar as there is no exposure to the general level of interest rates, and protection can be based on an entity without regard to a specific asset. Additionally, intermediate payments (that is, the periodic exchanges of increase or decrease in value of the reference asset) are not required.

Recap

Risk transfer	Default
Balance sheet	Off
Funding	Option: the credit protection buyer must fund the premium.
	Swap: the credit protection buyer's premium payment is funded via the swap payments.
Transaction credit risk	Swap or option: the credit protection buyer has credit risk to the credit protection seller.

Swap: the credit protection buyer has credit risk to the credit protection seller.

Option: the credit protection seller does not have any credit risk to the credit protection buyer once the premium has been paid.

Primary Applications

- Trading
- Funding
- Bank regulatory capital
- Leverage
- Concentration—credit limit management

Variations

Callable Step-Up Swap

A bank would like to reduce its regulatory capital requirement over a reporting period. They are considering using a credit default swap.

In order to achieve regulatory capital relief, the credit default swap must (among other things) be irrevocable and for the term of the underlying asset. Purchasing such protection is considered too costly. The bank may enter into a callable step-up swap.

A callable step-up swap has a stated term equal to that of the underlying asset. However, it is callable at the protection buyer's option. The cost of the protection is initially relatively low but increases dramatically after a short period of time (typically after the reporting date). The expectation is that the protection buyer will call the swap at the point in time when the cost increases. This trade meets the technical requirements for achieving credit capital relief, but is a short-dated transaction.

Credit Default Swap Option

A *credit default swap option*, or *credit default swaption*, is nothing more than an option to enter into a credit default swap at a fixed spread at a future time. The underlying reference credit can be either an index or an individual credit.

Payers have the option to buy protection via the credit default swap. As with all purchases of protection, payers are short the credit and benefit when spreads widen. On the other hand, *receivers* have the option to sell protection and go long the credit and, therefore, benefit when spreads tighten.

Options on single credits typically have a knockout feature that extinguishes the option when a credit event is called against the underlying credit. Therefore, entering into an option to purchase protection on a credit is reasonable if the expectation is that it will deteriorate but not default.

As with any option, these options have the same pros (leverage, limited losses on long positions) and cons (leverage, potentially unlimited losses on short positions) and can be used for hedging or to construct complex volatility strategies.

Recovery Swap

Recovery rate assumptions are critical to evaluating credit default products, and, therefore, market participants are exposed to the risk that the realized recovery rate varies significantly from their expectations when establishing a credit derivative position. Recent efforts to address recovery rate risk have focused on techniques that utilize CDSs with a fixed payout. The fixed payout effectively locks in the recovery assumption. These swaps are sometimes referred to as *digital default swaps* or, in the case of a zero recovery assumption, *zero strike swaps*.

A *recovery swap* is a package consisting of two offsetting CDSs: one with a fixed payout amount and the other with the now standard physical settlement process (the floating amount). The two swaps are structured to offset in every respect except the recovery amount upon default, thus, this structure is a play on the recovery amount assumption.

Recovery swap *buyers* are long the protection on a floating recovery basis and short the protection on a fixed recovery basis, therefore, benefiting when the recovery rate assumption increases. Conversely, recovery swap *sellers* benefit when the recovery rate assumption decreases.

Caution should be exercised when utilizing fixed recovery rate swaps as regards the event of default definition because of the possibility that soft credit events, which result in high recovery rates, may trigger payouts on digital swaps with low recovery rates.

Constant Maturity Credit Default Swap

A *constant maturity credit default swap* is a CDS in which the amount paid for the credit default protection (the fixed-rate payment) is periodically reset to reflect current market levels. By allowing the protection buyer (the *fixed-rate payer*) to effectively pay a *floating rate*, a market participant can express a view on the forward shape of the credit curve. The floating spread is expressed as a percentage of a benchmark CDS rate. The percentage (or *participation rate*) is negotiated at inception and remains constant through maturity of the trade. The benchmark (or *reference rate*) is for the term of the trade and can be either a single credit or an index.

For example, a market participant with a view that XYZ's credit curve is overly steep may enter into a constant maturity credit default swap (CMCDS) and pay 80% of the current five-year CDS rate for XYZ. At the reset dates (for example, semiannually), the spread is reset to 80% of the then-current five-year CDS spread for XYZ (ergo the *constant maturity*). The buyer in this example will have purchased credit default protection at a lower rate to the extent that the future five-year CDS rates do not rise as much as inferred by the spreads at the inception of the trade. If the market participants are wrong, they will ultimately pay more than if they had purchased a regular CDS. Additionally, insofar as CMCDS trades are a *floating rate* instrument, they have the benefit of showing relatively stable mark-to-markets and, therefore, lower P&L volatility.

All terms other than those related to the spread payment are the same as for a regular credit default swap and, therefore, the protection purchased in a CMCDS is the same as that of a regular CDS with the same credit events, credit event payments, and so forth.

The volume of CMCDS trades is expected to increase as the availability of publicly available unbiased price fixings for the reference credits increase.

Constant Spread Swap

Similar to the *recovery swaps* discussed previously, a *constant spread swap* is a package consisting of two offsetting CDSs: one a CMCDS and the other a regular CDS. The two swaps are structured to offset in every respect except the offsetting spread payments. This structure allows market participants to express a view as to the shape of the spread curve without regard to default. For example, if a market participant believes that spreads will widen more than is implied in the current CDS curve, he will receive a floating spread in the CMCDS and pay the fixed spread in a regular CDS. The credit event payments will offset in the event of a default.

Credit Spread Forward and Option

Unlike CDSs, which only pay out due to a "default" (or more precisely upon a credit event as defined in the trade confirmation), credit spread products pay out based on changes in the perceived credit quality of the reference credit as reflected in the spreads.

Spreads can be between either a reference credit and a risk-free rate or two different reference credits.

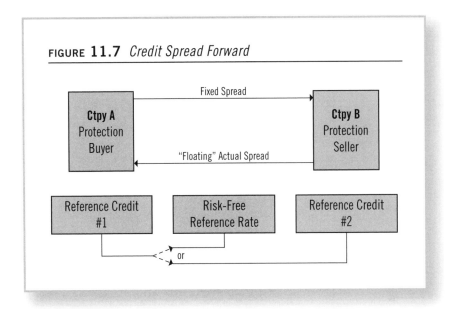

FIGURE **11.7** *Credit Spread Forward*

Basic Mechanics

Credit Spread Forward

Ctpy A agrees to pay a fixed spread to Ctpy B.

Ctpy B agrees to pay a floating spread (that is, the actual observed spread) to Ctpy A.

Payments, which may be netted, are calculated as

$$\text{Spread} \times \text{Leverage factor (usually } DV01) \times \text{Notional}$$

$DV01$ (dollar value of 1 basis point) is an indication of the change in price for a small change in yield.

Insofar as Ctpy A in our example is protected against a deterioration in the credit quality of the reference asset (that is, the spread widens), it is considered the protection buyer for comparison to other products discussed.

Credit Spread Option

As with any call option, the buyer receives a payment when the spread at exercise is higher than the strike.

$$\text{Call payment} = (\text{Spread @ Maturity} - \text{Strike}) \times \text{Leverage factor}$$
$$\text{usually } DV01) \times \text{Notional}$$

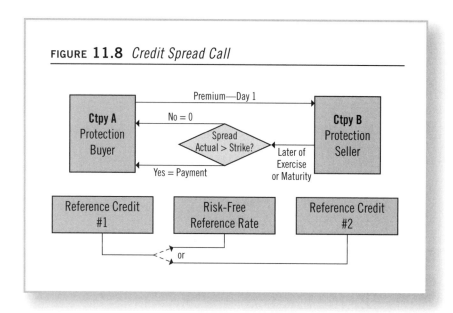

FIGURE **11.8** *Credit Spread Call*

Note that as the spread increases, the credit quality of the reference asset is deteriorating. Therefore, insofar as the buyer of the credit spread call benefits from a deterioration in the credit quality of the reference asset, it is considered the protection buyer for comparison to the other products discussed.

As with any put option, the seller must make a payment when the spread at exercise is lower than the strike.

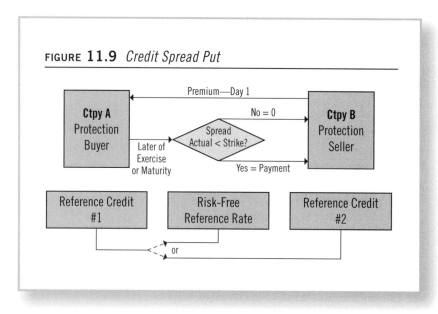

FIGURE **11.9** *Credit Spread Put*

Put payment = (Strike − Spread @ maturity) × Leverage factor
(usually $DV01$) × Notional

Note that as the spread decreases, the credit quality of the reference asset is improving. Therefore, insofar as the seller of the credit spread put benefits from a deterioration in the credit quality of the reference asset (that is, it has received a premium without making a payout), it is considered the protection buyer for comparison to the other products discussed.

As with any other option, credit spread options can be structured as *exotics*, such as:

❏ **Knock-Ins**—where the option does not become effective until a barrier level is achieved (for example, spreads must widen by 20 bps).

❏ **Knock-Outs**—where the option extinguishes if a barrier level is crossed (for example, if spreads tighten by 10 bps).

Recap

Risk Transfer	Spread
Balance Sheet	Off
Funding	Forward: none
	Options: the option buyer must fund the premium payment
Transaction credit risk	Forward: Ctpy A and Ctpy B have credit risk to each other
	Option: the option buyer (either call or put) has credit risk to the option seller. The option seller does not have any credit risk to the buyer once the premium has been paid.

Applications

Spread products are targeted to counterparties who want to express a view as to the direction of spreads but do not expect default.

However, the need for spread products diminishes as the liquidity of the CDS market improves. With the increasing number of reference assets with significant liquidity, it is now possible to efficiently express a view as to spreads by entering into a CDS and then closing out the position when spread changes are reflected in the CDS price.

Nonetheless, spread products still suit the needs of some market participants (for example, they receive favorable treatment versus default products in some regulatory capital regimes) so they continue to represent a small and proportionately decreasing volume of the credit derivative market.[5]

Asset Swap Option

As the name implies, an asset swap option is an option on an asset swap. These *asset swaptions* are sometimes referred to as *synthetic lending facilities* insofar as the cash flows resemble those of a revolving credit facility.

In a revolving credit facility, the borrower pays a fee for the right to borrow at a predetermined spread in the future (see **FIGURE 11.10**).

In an asset swaption, the *borrower* is most likely a bank, and the *asset*

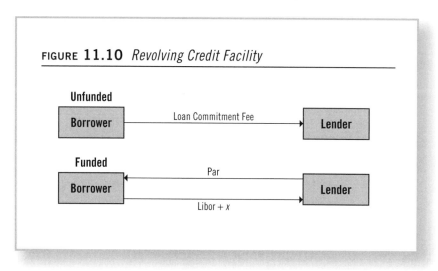

FIGURE **11.10** *Revolving Credit Facility*

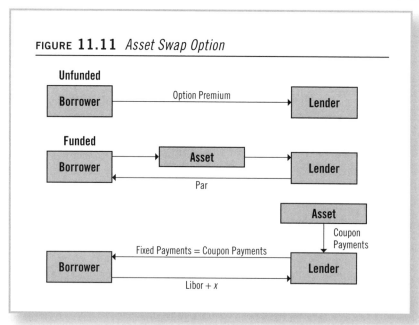

FIGURE **11.11** *Asset Swap Option*

that is swapped is a revolving credit facility from a client. Thus, the *borrower* bank has hedged itself to the credit risk of the client to whom they have provided the revolving credit line.

This option is typically triggered by the funding to the client.

As with traditional lending facilities, these synthetic lending facilities have a regulatory capital risk weight of 50% while unfunded and a 100% risk weight when funded.

Credit-Linked Notes

Credit-linked notes are notes with credit derivatives embedded in them. Any type of credit derivative can be used, but typically credit default options are used.

Ctpy B, the protection seller (also referred to as the *investor*) purchases the credit-linked notes.

Ctpy A, the protection buyer (also referred to as the *issuer*) makes periodic interest payments that reflect the premium.

If the reference credit does not have a credit event, Ctpy A will pay the full face value of the note to Ctpy B at maturity. If however, the reference credit does have a credit event, Ctpy A will reduce the payment to Ctpy B by the credit event payment amount.

Although credit-linked notes typically have credit default options embedded in them, they may also include payoffs linked to an index or have coupons that are a function of rating levels (for example, coupons decrease if rating deteriorates).

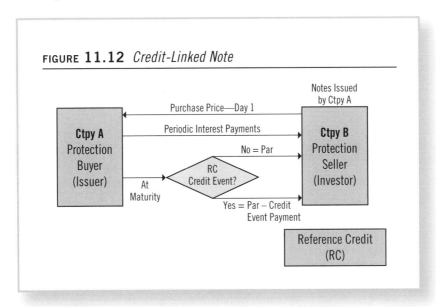

FIGURE 11.12 *Credit-Linked Note*

Applications

Entities that are not allowed to engage in derivative transactions can participate in the credit derivatives market via credit-linked notes.

Since credit-linked notes are funded up front, the protection buyer has no credit exposure to the protection seller and, therefore, no use of internal credit lines. This makes credit-linked notes an effective structure for counterparties who are either poorly rated or to whom the issuer already has significant exposure.

Recap

Risk transfer	Default
Balance sheet	On
Funding	Ctpy B, the investor, must fund the note purchase.
Transaction credit risk	Ctpy A, the protection buyer, does not have any credit risk to Ctpy B once the purchase has been funded.
	Ctpy B, the protection seller, has credit risk to Ctpy A, the protection buyer.

Principal-Protected Notes

Principal-protected notes are a specialized form of credit-linked notes wherein the investor is guaranteed to receive all the principal. They are targeted to investors who have limited risk-taking ability, such as insurance companies.

Although principal-protected notes are relatively rare, their description is included here to introduce two techniques that are critical to the structured products discussed later in this chapter: the use of special purpose vehicles (SPVs) and the investment of cash proceeds in risk-free securities.

Basic Mechanics

Ctpy B, the protection seller, purchases the principal-protected notes from an SPV (see **FIGURE 11.13**).

SPVs are independent, nonconsolidated, bankruptcy-remote legal entities established for the express (and typically sole) purpose of issuing the notes. The SPV uses the proceeds of the notes to purchase highly rated zero-coupon bonds (typically U.S. Treasuries) that will accrete to the notional value of the notes by maturity date. The remaining funds will be used to partially fund the interest payments on the notes (typically also via zero-coupon bonds). These interest payments are supplemented with the cash flows from the periodic payments received from the protection buyer (the credit default option premium).

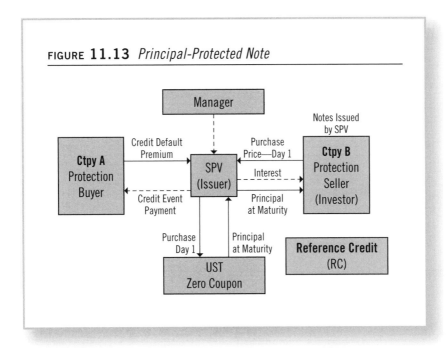

FIGURE **11.13** *Principal-Protected Note*

Ctpy A, the protection buyer, makes periodic swap payments to the SPV representing the premium for the embedded credit default option.

The SPV makes periodic interest payments on the notes to Ctpy B unless there is a credit event on the reference credit. If a credit event occurs on the reference credit, the SPV will reduce or eliminate the interest payments on the notes and a credit event payment will be made to Ctpy A.

Nonetheless, under all circumstances, Ctpy B will be repaid the entire principal on the notes via the zero-coupon bonds.

First-to-Default Basket Options and Swaps

First-to-default basket options and swaps work essentially the same as a single-name credit default option/swap except that the credit event payment is triggered when a credit event occurs to the first of a defined group of reference assets.

Basic Mechanics

Baskets typically have between three and ten reference credits. These credits are agreed upon between the protection buyer and the protection seller. The protection seller is exposed to each of the reference credits in the basket for the full amount but only for the first credit event among all the reference credits. For example: assume a trade notional of $10 million

TABLE **11.1** *Credit Derivative Product Recap*

| PRODUCTS | CHARACTERISTICS | |
	RISK TRANSFER	BALANCE SHEET
Asset Swap	Default	Protection Seller has the Bond On Balance Sheet. Swap is Off Balance Sheet.
Total Return Swap	Total Return	Off
Credit Default Option	Default	Off
Credit Default Swap	Default	Off
Credit Spread Forward	Spread	Off
Credit Spread Option	Spread	Off
Credit-Linked Note	Default	On
Principal-Protected Notes	Default (limited)	Notes are On Balance Sheet. Swap is Off Balance Sheet.
Collateralized Debt Obligations	Total Return	Notes are On Balance Sheet. Swap is Off Balance Sheet.

FUNDING	TRANSACTION CREDIT RISK
The Protection Seller must fund the purchase of the underlying asset.	Both parties have risk to each other on the interest-rate swap.
The Protection Seller (the party Long the Reference Asset) via periodic payments	Both parties have credit risk to each other.
The Protection Buyer must fund the premium payment.	The Protection Buyer has credit risk to the Protection Seller.
	The Protection Seller does not have any credit risk to the Protection Buyer after the premium is paid.
The Protection Buyer's premium payment is funded via the swap payments.	Both parties have credit risk to each other, though the Protection Buyer's credit risk to the Protection Seller is higher.
None	Both parties have credit risk to each other.
The Option Buyer must fund the premium payment.	The Option Buyer (either put or call) has credit risk to the Option Seller.
	The Option Seller does not have credit risk to the Option Buyer after the premium is paid.
The Protection Seller (the investor) must fund the Note purchase.	The Protection Buyer does not have any credit risk to the Protection Seller once the purchase is funded.
	The Protection Seller has credit risk to the Protection Buyer.
The Protection Sellers (the investors) must fund the Note purchase.	The Protection Buyer does not have any credit risk to the Protection Seller once the purchase is funded.
	Both parties have credit risk to the SPV, but it should be remote.
The Protection Sellers (the investors) must fund the Note purchase.	Note holders (and swap counterparties, if any) have credit risk to the SPV, but it should be remote.

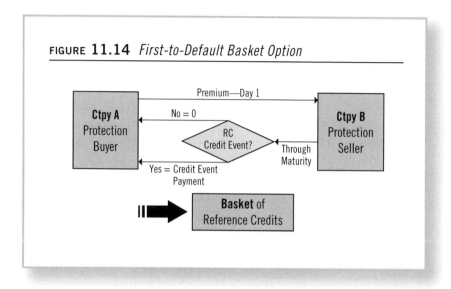

FIGURE **11.14** *First-to-Default Basket Option*

on four reference credits: A, B, C and D. The protection seller will have to make a credit event payment based on a notional of $10 million when whichever of the reference credits has the first credit event, if any. However, the protection seller is exposed to *only* the first default, after which the trade expires.

Settlement options and procedures are the same as for single-name credit default options or swaps.

The premium can be paid either as an annuity in a swap format or as a single payment in an option format.

Generally, the premium will be higher for:
- ❑ A larger number of reference credits in the basket
- ❑ Lower-quality reference credits
- ❑ Lower correlation among the reference credits

The intuition for the first two of these relationships is straightforward: if the protection seller is exposed to the default of any of the names in the basket, then the more names there are in the basket and the lower their rating (the higher their probability of defaulting), then the more risk is being assumed and the higher the compensation should be for assuming the risk.

Whenever there is more than one reference credit within a credit derivative, the correlations between and among them becomes a critical valuation parameter. But lowering the correlation means that the basket is becoming more diversified, and isn't diversification a positive thing?

Increasing diversification in an investment portfolio is a desirable goal in that it reduces the likelihood of multiple defaults occurring simultane-ously, thus, reducing the likelihood of experiencing a large loss (*Don't put all your eggs in one basket*). Assume that you are investing $1 million in each of ten companies. If one of the ten companies defaults, you are ex-posed to a $1 million loss, only 10% of your total investment. By being uncorrelated, the likelihood of having multiple defaults is low, and the likelihood of having all ten companies default is extremely unlikely.

Now assume that you are investing your $10 million in a first-to-default basket. Increasing diversification increases the likelihood of hav-ing *a* loss. Any one loss within a default basket transaction exposes the protection seller to the full notional of the trade, $10 million in this example. In this context, higher diversification means there is a higher likelihood of experiencing a loss for the full amount. Therefore, the less correlated (more diversified) the basket is, the more risk there is, and the higher the premium should be.

By using probability of default, recovery, and correlation assumptions for the reference credits, the probability of default for the basket trans-action can be estimated and used to benchmark the value to alternative investments with equivalent risk.

Variations

Nth-to-Default Basket Options and Swaps

The previous section describes *first-to-default baskets*, but the struc-ture can be used as well for second-, third-, fourth-to-default, and so on, though there currently is limited liquidity in these products.

Collateralized Debt Obligations

Collateralized debt obligations (CDOs) are repackaging structures used to securitize credit products. The underlying financial engineering technol-ogy is an extension of that used for collateralized mortgage obligations. The objective of structuring CDOs, as with all financial engineering, is to convert a series of cash inflows into a series of cash outflows such that the value of the outflows is greater than the value of the inflows. CDOs come in two basic varieties defined by the underlying asset:

❑ Collateralized bond obligations (CBOs) date from about 1990.
❑ Collateralized loan obligations (CLOs) date from about 1996.

The primary objective of CBOs and CLOs was to remove assets from the balance sheet and possibly achieve regulatory capital relief. Thus, they are known as *balance sheet CDOs*. Originating banks would receive regu-

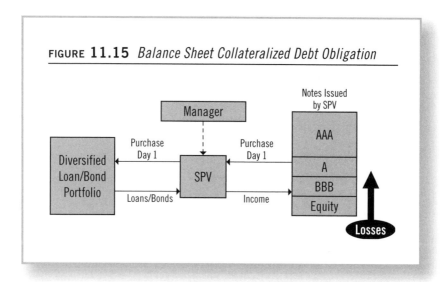

FIGURE 11.15 *Balance Sheet Collateralized Debt Obligation*

latory capital relief to the extent that the amount of first loss it retained (via ownership of the equity tranche) was less than 8%. The typical level retained would be in the range of 3% or less. In the case of CLOs, the originating bank would also typically retain the servicing of the loans, thereby earning fee income and preserving some level of confidentiality of the underlying assets.

Basic Mechanics

SPVs are independent, nonconsolidated, bankruptcy-remote legal entities established for the express (and typically sole) purpose of receiving the income stream from the assets and distributing it to the holders of the notes that it has issued.

The notes are issued in tranches, which are structured such that the lowest tranche is the first to absorb losses. Any losses in excess of the notional of the lowest tranche will be absorbed by the second lowest tranche, and so forth. Accordingly, the higher level tranches are less likely to experience a credit loss. The lowest, *equity*, tranche is usually retained by the sponsoring bank.

Moody's, S&P, and Fitch have each developed their own model for evaluating CDOs. A full discussion of their similarities and differences is beyond the scope of this chapter, but full descriptions of these models are readily available on their Web sites.

The ratings of the tranches are a function of:

❑ *The quality of the underlying assets.* The quality of the underlying assets is determined by ratings. If an asset does not already have a ratings agency rating, either (1) the originating financial institution will have

FIGURE 11.16 *CDO Tranches*

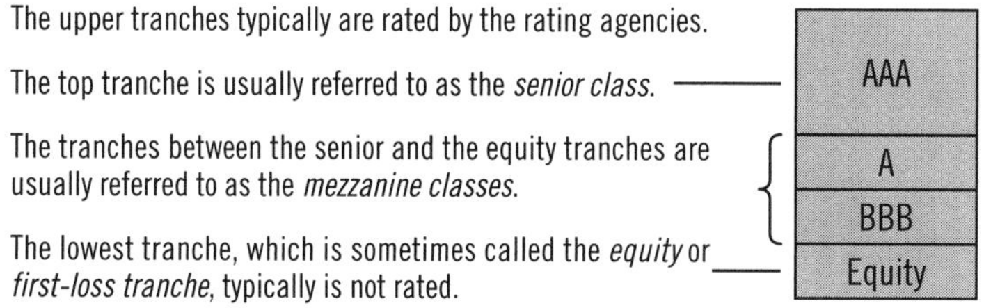

The upper tranches typically are rated by the rating agencies.

The top tranche is usually referred to as the *senior class.* ——— [AAA]

The tranches between the senior and the equity tranches are usually referred to as the *mezzanine classes.* { [A] [BBB]

The lowest tranche, which is sometimes called the *equity* or *first-loss tranche*, typically is not rated. —— [Equity]

to demonstrate that its internal ratings are consistently applied, in which case the internal ratings can be mapped to the ratings agency equivalent rating or (2) the asset will have to be given a *shadow rating* by the ratings agency for the purpose of the CDO.

❑ *The diversification of the underlying assets.* Moody's and S&P assign assets to regional and industry categories. Fitch uses equity correlations as a proxy.

❑ *The subordination structure of the tranches.* The larger the size of the tranches below a given tranche, the more protection against incurring a loss it has and the higher its rating.

❑ *Any additional credit enhancement.* Additional credit enhancement can be achieved by purchasing credit insurance or by entering into a credit derivative.

The CDO SPV distributes losses from the bottom tranche upward and income from the top tranches downward (see **FIGURE 11.17**).

There are literally infinite possibilities for creating product by combining the basic CDO structure with interest rate, FX, and credit derivatives. For example, FX swaps can be used to convert portfolio cash flows from their base currency into a different currency that is more attractive to an investor.

Fully Funded Synthetic CDO

Fully funded synthetic CDOs made their U.S. debut in 1997. *Fully funded* refers to the fact that the notional of the notes issued is approximately the same as the underlying assets. It is referred to as *synthetic* because instead

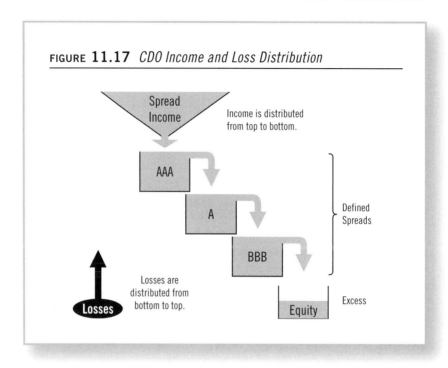

FIGURE 11.17 *CDO Income and Loss Distribution*

of incurring the expense of selling the underlying loans to the SPV, the originating bank enters into a portfolio CDS with the SPV.

Basic Mechanics

As with the balance sheet CDO, a fully funded synthetic CDO establishes an SPV, which issues notes in a series of tranches (see **FIGURE 11.18**). However, unlike a balance sheet CDO, instead of using the proceeds from issuing the notes to purchase the underlying loan or bond portfolio, the SPV invests the proceeds in high-quality collateral (typically U.S. Treasuries) and enters into a CDS with the sponsoring bank on the underlying portfolio. This approach is significantly less expensive (and faster) than actually selling and transferring the underlying loans or bonds to the SPV.

The interest earned on the collateral plus the CDS premiums from the sponsoring bank are used to make interest payments on the notes.

If a credit event occurs, the SPV will sell some of the collateral to make the credit event payment to the sponsoring bank and inform the note holders of the lowest tranche still outstanding (the equity tranche first) that their notional balance has been decreased.

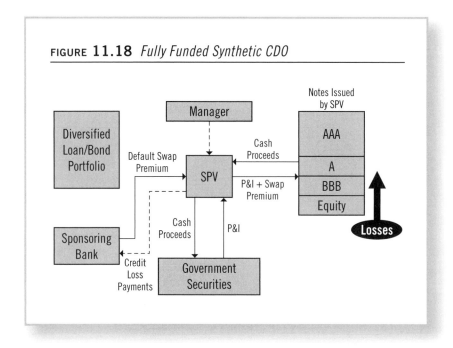

FIGURE **11.18** *Fully Funded Synthetic CDO*

Partially Funded Synthetic CDO

The first partially funded synthetic CDO was the Bistro issued by JP Morgan in December 1997. The term *partially funded* refers to the fact that the notional amount of the notes issued by the SPV is significantly less than that of the underlying portfolio of assets. This structure is achieved by utilizing the innovation of a *super-senior tranche*.

Basic Mechanics

In a partially funded CDO, a super-senior tranche is created that has an effective rating higher than AAA (see **FIGURE 11.19**). This tranche constitutes a very high percentage (upwards of 80%) of the structure. Typically, only the mezzanine tranches (which may now include AAA) are sold with the proceeds used to purchase high-quality collateral (for example, U.S. Treasuries). The SPV enters into a credit default swap with the sponsoring bank, which covers only the loss levels that correspond to the notes that are sold. For example, if the notional of the underlying portfolio is $100 million, the equity tranche is $5 million and the super-senior tranche is $80 million, then the CDS with the sponsoring bank would cover losses above 5% up to 20% for total loss coverage of up to 15%.

The sponsoring bank typically retains both the equity and the super-

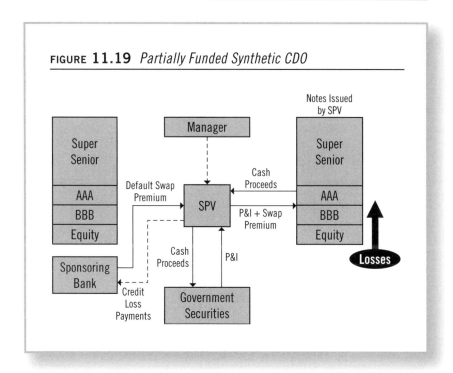

FIGURE 11.19 *Partially Funded Synthetic CDO*

senior tranches. This is the case because no one wants to buy them: the first-loss equity tranche is too risky and the super-senior tranche is so riskless, that the return that can be offered on it would be insufficient to justify funding the purchase.

Synthetic Arbitrage CDO

Synthetic arbitrage CDOs introduced two significant innovations to the CDO structure: the use of credit derivatives to
   ❑ artificially create the pool of reference assets, and
   ❑ transfer the risk of the super-senior tranche.

Basic Mechanics

The first important innovation in a synthetic arbitrage CDO is the artificial creation of the reference pool by the use of credit derivatives (see **FIGURE 11.20**). It was no longer necessary to locate or create an appropriate pool of underlying loans or bonds. The use of credit derivatives (typically CDSs) provided significant flexibility to quickly create an optimal portfolio of raw material. The reduction in ramp-up time made it easier to structure the transaction and issue the notes in a format that would quickly meet investor demand.

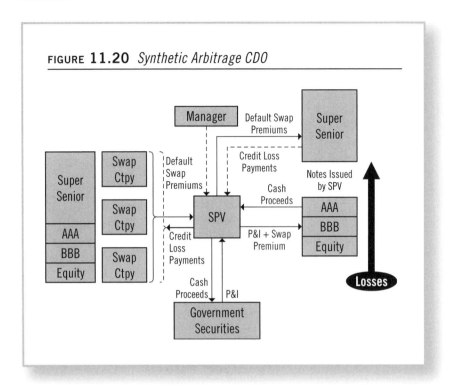

FIGURE **11.20** *Synthetic Arbitrage CDO*

The second important innovation was the use of a credit derivative to transfer the risk of the super-senior tranche to an investor. The super-senior tranche's risk is very low and whatever spread it could potentially earn would be inadequate to compensate an investor to fund its purchase. However, investors were willing to accept a premium payment to enter into a CDS on the super-senior tranche. The payments were extremely small, but without the need to fund and the extremely low risk, investors looked at these payments as close to being free money.

The relatively inexpensive cost of the CDS protection on the super-senior tranche is the key to the economics of this structure: the additional net spread versus credit default protection sold allows for increased returns on the mezzanine and equity tranches (see **FIGURE 11.21**).

Initially, CDOs were *static*—the composition of the portfolio was established at inception and it remained essentially unchanged through maturity. However, unexpectedly high credit losses of 2001–2002 and the increased sophistication of the product resulted in the increasing use of *managed* CDOs.

As compared to a static CDO, the manager of a managed CDO can:

❑ Trade the assets in the portfolio up to a defined level (for example, 5% per year) in order to

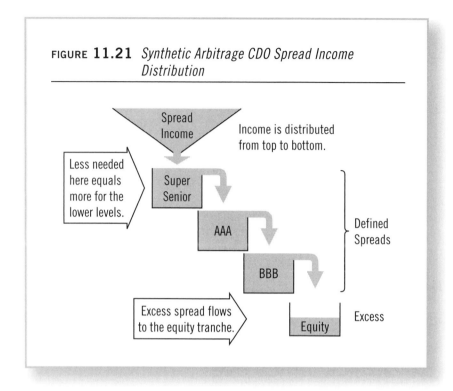

FIGURE **11.21** *Synthetic Arbitrage CDO Spread Income Distribution*

—Sell swaps that have increased in value
—Buy additional protection on deteriorating names
—Replace positions to generate wider spreads
❑ Decide on the timing for liquidating defaulted securities to try to optimize the recovery rate

The combination of the potential for meaningful amounts of excess spread to be earned by the owners of the equity tranche and the ability to manage the portfolio led to the development of professional CDO managers who own the equity tranche.

This is a moral hazard for the managers who have a fiduciary responsibility to all the note holders but also have the potential to earn excess spread from the equity tranche. The concern is that the managers will restructure the portfolio to their own advantage to the detriment of the other tranche owners. The owners of the senior tranches prefer to have a diversified portfolio that has a higher likelihood of having a small loss, which could be absorbed by the equity tranche (see **FIGURE 11.22**). On the other hand, the owners of the equity tranche would prefer to have a less diversified portfolio with a lower probability of having a larger loss. CDOs typically now address this moral hazard by the use of reserve pools

FIGURE **11.22** *The Impact of Correlation on the Probability of a Default and the Size of the Default*

	Probability of a Default	Probability of the Default Being Large
Low Correlation/High Diversification	Higher	Lower
High Correlation/Low Diversification	Lower	Higher

that accumulate excess spread to offset excess credit losses. In this manner, only excess spread net of losses will accrue to the equity tranche.

Resecuritizations

Resecuritizations are synthetic CDOs in which the portfolio of assets from which the tranches are created for investors is a series of individual tranches.

Basic Mechanics

The tranches that comprise the underlying portfolio can be other CDO tranches (in which case the transaction is referred to as a CDO^2 or *CDO-squared*) or any other structured finance securities tranche, such as mortgage-backed securities, commercial mortgage-backed securities or asset-backed securities.

The key to the additional value created by securitizing assets that are already securitized is in the additional diversification achieved. However, although liquidity in credit derivatives continues to improve, a limited number of reference credits constitute the majority of the underlying reference credits in CDOs. As a result, a reference credit will appear in tranches from multiple CDOs, resulting in significant overlap of the reference credits in the ultimate underlying portfolio of a CDO-squared transaction.

These structures can run the full range of CDO variations (for exam-

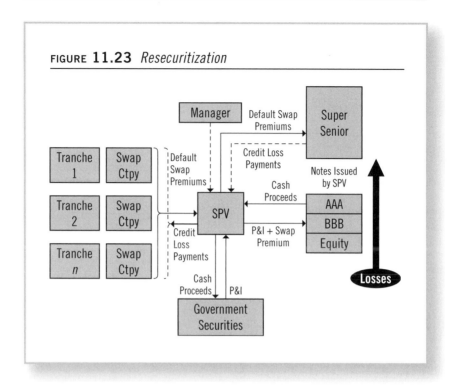

FIGURE **11.23** *Resecuritization*

ple, funded/unfunded, cash/physical settle, and others) and provide the ultimate flexibility for structuring notes that meet investor demands.

Index Products

In 2003, two groups of international financial institutions developed and marketed competing indexes of CDS prices. They have since merged, resulting in two families of indexes: the Dow Jones CDX (for North America and emerging markets) and the Dow Jones iTraxx (for Europe and Asia/Pacific).

The two primary indexes are the North American Investment Grade and the European Investment Grade, each consisting of 125 equally weighted CDSs for a range of terms, five and ten years being the most liquid. Every six months, the composition of each index is reviewed and, if necessary, changed to reflect the current CDS market's most liquid reference credits resulting in a new on-the-run series. Therefore, unlike other financial indexes, CDS indexes are traded based on a specific series with the composition varying among the outstanding series.

These indexes assume that the underlying CDS have only bankruptcy and failure to pay as credit events and are physically settled.

New indexes and subindexes are constantly under development.

FIGURE **11.24** *Subindexes*

NORTH AMERICA	EUROPE
Industrials	Industrials
Consumer	Consumer
Energy	Energy
Financial	Financial (sr. and sub.)
TMT (technology, media, and telecommunications)	TMT
	Nonfinancial
	Autos

FIGURE **11.25** *Additional Indexes (Number of Underlying CDS)*

North American High Yield	(100)
European Corporates	(100)
European Hi Vol	(30)
European Crossover	(30)
Emerging Markets	(14)
Asia (except Japan)	(30)
Japan	(50)
Australia	(30)

FIGURE 11.24 lists the North American and European Investment Grade subindexes, and **FIGURE 11.25** lists additional indexes other than the North American and European Investment Grade. These tables reflect the universe of indexes as of the writing of this chapter; however, liquidity levels vary greatly with the North American and European Investment Grade indexes the most liquid.

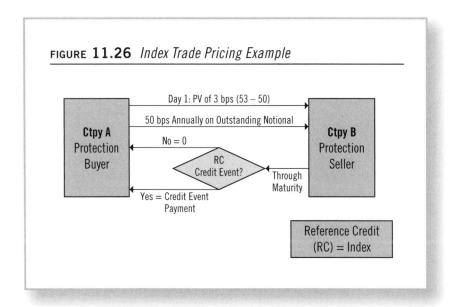

FIGURE 11.26 *Index Trade Pricing Example*

Basic Mechanics

Index trades are executed in the form of CDSs with the index as the reference credit. Each index series has a fixed spread for the life of the index. Current pricing is reflected by exchanging the present value of the difference between the current price and the fixed spread. In the example in **FIGURE 11.26**, the fixed spread on the index is 50 bps per annum, and the current price is 53 bps. Therefore, the credit protection buyer must make an up-front payment to the credit protection seller equal to the present value of (53 − 50) 3 bps. Thereafter, the protection buyer must pay the annual fixed spread.

Alternatively, if the current price was 46 bps, the credit protection seller would have to make a payment to the credit protection buyer for the present value of (50 − 46) 4 bps.

Upon a default by one of the reference credits in the index,

❏ Protection buyer delivers securities with face amount equal to (1/125) 0.8% of the notional of the trade to the protection seller.

❏ Protection seller pays 0.8% of the notional of the trade to the protection buyer.

❏ The notional on the trade is reduced by 0.8%.

Tranches

Indexes can trade as a whole or as standardized tranches (see **FIGURE 11.27**). These tranches approximate those of a CDO and are described in terms of percentage of loss (for example, the 3%–7% tranche of the

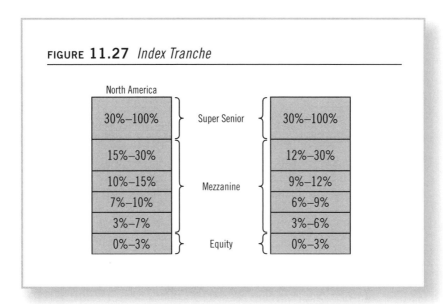

FIGURE **11.27** *Index Tranche*

North American Investment Grade Index covers losses on the index greater than 3%—the attachment point—up to 7%—the detachment point). The ability to trade tranches provides significant opportunities to structure customized exposures.

Tranche Pricing

The pricing convention for the equity tranche is to pay a fixed amount up front (expressed as a percentage of notional) and a spread paid annually (for example, 40% and 500 bps).

The pricing convention for the mezzanine tranches is to pay a spread annually (for example, 300 bps).

Trading Strategies

Index trading strategies can be either passive (buy and hold) or active (delta hedging).

Delta-hedging strategies are similar to standard option techniques. In the case of CDS indexes, delta is the change in tranche spread for a small change in the index spread. Delta is also referred to as *leverage* (for example, if the delta of the 0%–3% tranche is 12, then it is expected to move 12 times as much as the index and, therefore, an investment in the 0%–3% tranche will have 12 times the price sensitivity of an investment in the index).

Tranche Dynamics

The valuation and trading of tranches requires highly sophisticated modeling skills. This section will briefly describe only a few of the key dynamics of tranche valuation.

Correlation

As with the basket trades described earlier in the chapter, the value of the indexes will be a function of the probability of default and recovery assumption for each of the constituent reference credits in the index and the assumption for the default correlation among all the reference credits. The default correlation among the constituent reference credits within the CDS index is the key valuation assumption:

Correlation is to indexes what volatility is to options.

As option traders are said to *trade volatility*, credit index tranche traders are said to *trade correlation*.

An increase in correlation will cause an

❏ Increase in the expected loss in the senior tranches and, therefore, the theoretical value of the protection will increase.

❏ Decrease in the expected loss in the equity tranche and, therefore, the theoretical value of the protection will decrease.

A decrease in correlation would have the opposite effects. Refer back to Figure 11.22 and the discussion regarding moral hazard within the synthetic arbitrage CDO section for the reasoning behind this relationship.

Similar to option-implied volatility, the implied correlations of the tranches typically vary within an index resulting in a *smile* (that is, the actual correlation that will be realized among the 125 credits in the index must be the same regardless of the particular tranche, yet the correlations implied by the models based on actual market prices for the tranches are not the same).

The Effects of Time

The price sensitivity of the passage of time differs among the tranches. Everything else held constant, as the index approaches maturity, the likelihood of the index experiencing losses large enough to affect the higher tranches decreases. Therefore, the value of the higher tranches will decrease relatively faster than the lower tranches. Trading strategies with long-short higher versus lower tranches will need to rebalance the hedge if for no other reason than the passage of time.

Jump-to-Default Risk

The models used to evaluate basket transactions assume *orderly defaults*: the weakest credit (that is, the credit with the highest spread) defaults first and the credit deteriorates in an orderly manner before defaulting. *Jump-to-default risk* is the risk that a credit other than the credit with the highest spread is the first to default, and it does so without first showing deterioration in the spread. This is a concern because delta hedging is partial hedging, and its effectiveness is predicated on continually adjusting the hedge ratio. As a credit within a basket deteriorates, the delta hedge ratios would change and would shift more protection against the deteriorating credit. The goal is to fully hedge the deteriorating credit by the time it defaults. If the credit jumps to default (that is, there is no orderly deterioration), the risk manager will not have adjusted the hedge ratio appropriately, and the defaulted credit will not be fully covered, resulting in a loss.

Chapter Notes

1. Refer to www.bis.org for up-to-date detailed documentation on regulatory capital guidelines.

2. 2004 British Bankers Association credit derivatives survey.

3. Refer to www.isda.org.

4. Twenty percent of the market volume as per the 2004 British Bankers Association survey.

5. 2004 British Bankers Association survey.

INDEX

PROFESSIONAL
DEVELOPMENT
QUALIFIED ACTIVITY
7.5 CREDIT HOURS

This book qualifies for 7.5 PD credits under the guidelines of the CFA Institute Professional Development Program. Please visit www.cfainstitute.org/memresources/pdprogram for more information.

Bloomberg L.P., founded in 1981, is a global information services, news, and media company. Headquartered in New York, the company has sales and news operations worldwide.

Bloomberg, serving customers on six continents, holds a unique position within the financial services industry by providing an unparalleled range of features in a single package known as the BLOOMBERG PROFESSIONAL® service. By addressing the demand for investment performance and efficiency through an exceptional combination of information, analytic, electronic trading, and Straight Through Processing tools, Bloomberg has built a worldwide customer base of corporations, issuers, financial intermediaries, and institutional investors.

BLOOMBERG NEWS®, founded in 1990, provides stories and columns on business, general news, politics, and sports to leading newspapers and magazines throughout the world. BLOOMBERG TELEVISION®, a 24-hour business and financial news network, is produced and distributed globally in seven languages. BLOOMBERG RADIO℠ is an international radio network anchored by flagship station BLOOMBERG® 1130 (WBBR-AM) in New York.

In addition to the BLOOMBERG PRESS® line of books, Bloomberg publishes *BLOOMBERG MARKETS®* magazine. To learn more about Bloomberg, call a sales representative at:

London:	+44-20-7330-7500
New York:	+1-212-318-2000
Tokyo:	+81-3-3201-8900

FOR IN-DEPTH MARKET INFORMATION and news, visit the Bloomberg Web site at **www.bloomberg.com**, which draws from the news and power of the BLOOMBERG PROFESSIONAL® service and Bloomberg's host of media products to provide high-quality news and information in multiple languages on stocks, bonds, currencies, and commodities.

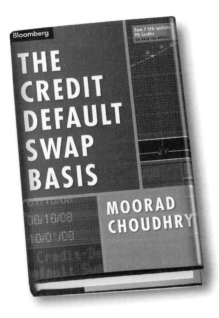